M A S T E R P I E C E S

PERFORMANCE
ARCHITECTURE + DESIGN

MASTERPIECES

CHRIS VAN UFFELEN

PERFORMANCE
ARCHITECTURE + DESIGN

PREFACE.

Theaters, philharmonic orchestras, concert halls and opera houses are among the most topical construction projects of our times. Many metropolises and many medium-sized and small communities are complementing their cultural infrastructure by adding buildings for the performing arts or by renewing historical structures. The acoustics and stage technology are brought up to par with modern requirements, the management utilities (security and air conditioning) are updated, and comfort considerably increased for visitors. Prestigious objects of cities and states, these buildings not only have very attractive interior designs but also shape the cityscape with their unique architecture. At the same time, theaters and concert halls are among the few building types who have not strayed far from their ancient origins. While sacral buildings have undergone substantial changes from antique temples and medieval basilica, whose basic shape served different purposes in antiquity, to modern churches, the buildings for the performing arts remained closely connected to their Greek origins. However, there are two essential differences – firstly, Greek theaters were incorporated into the landscape by utilizing natural slopes for their seating, and secondly, they did not have roofs.

The theater of Epidauros (early 3rd century BC, ill.) with its impressive tiers of seating in a more than semicircular shape includes the elementary features of a theater building: the orchestra (a round stage with an altar at its center), and the preserved foundations of the skene (the building used for the storage of props and costumes). The generally rather plain wooden skene was occasionally decorated with a hyposkenion, i.e. an architectural front wall, or by a painted stage setting with illusionary architecture, depending on the performance. The entrance was located between the skene and the rows of seating. The lacking roofs of Greek theaters were found in the Greek odeons, usually smaller buildings that served as concert halls.

In ancient Rome, theaters were constructed as structural designs independent of their surroundings. The wings on the side of the proscenium, which now served as the stage with the orchestra located in front, created a connection between the architecturally designed scena frons and the tiers of seats. Thus the spatial arrangement was preserved, while its use was changed and the structural construction of the building as well as the peripheral enclosure of the stage area turned the largely independent sections into a cohesive building.

During Medieval Times no new theaters were constructed, as in those days church crossings, stairs of church façades and mobile or improvised stages were used. In the Renaissance theater construction was a direct continuation of the antique archetype. The most important innovation, however, was surely the roofing of the entire building structure (1491 in Ferrara, burned down in 1532). The plays were performed on shallow stages, while the auditorium was architecturally embellished. One of the most impressive examples is the Teatro Olimpico in Vicenza, whose construction was started in 1580 by Palladio and whose essential interior design was completed in 1583 by Scamozzi in the Mannerism style. Perspectively reduced alleys extend into the depth of the stage from the illusionary architecture of the antique scena frons, creating an impression of a city as a fitted stage setting. At Jacob van Campen's Amsterdam theater this spatial illusion is an almost free-standing small architecture. The illusionary architectural design of stages was initially set up with a central perspective effect (Giacomo Torelli) then segments of diagonally positioned buildings were added (Ferdinando Galli da Bibiena). Van Campen's Palladian Baroque building also features galleries, which were used in earlier buildings, for example at Shakespeare's Globe Theatre, which was constructed in 1599 on the south bank of the Thames in London. As opposed to the predominant design of the era, this building was round (or octagonal), with three floors and while its interior was not roofed its stage was roofed. Similar to van Campen's building, it was a civic theater, while in subsequent eras royal buildings dominated. Comfortable galleries and boxes were to become standard features of baroque theaters, while the auditoriums of public buildings remained free of seats. At court theaters, however, the parquet furnished with seats was often the most exclusively seating. With a proscenium (a frame that surrounds and separates the stage like a picture), proscenium galleries, main curtain, a recessed orchestra pit and real backdrops as well as a suitably high theater building this finally resulted in the zograscope-style stage design that remains widely popular to this day. At the same time, stagecraft also advanced rapidly with the now elaborate theater productions (including mobile prospects and stages).

During Rococo and Neoclassicism theater construction matched the prevailing styles, while the Théâtre Feydeau in Paris by Jacques Legrand and Jacques Molinos featured the rounded façade that reflected the rounded auditorium and that came to dominate the Dresden opera house of Gottfried Semper (1841 Neocinquecento, 1871 Baroque Revival). The elevated stage tower was propagated by the theater specialists Fellner & Helmer. Their firm (1873 to 1919) built around 50 theaters, primarily in eastern Europe. Frank Matcham in Great Britain was similarly specialized with a greater range of styles. The growing importance of performing arts buildings as representative bourgeois structures led to the construction of the Paris opera in 1875. The key building of the Baroque Revival era by Charles Garnier with a magnificent staircase and foyer served socializing functions and constituted the point de vue of two axes of city redevelopment by Baron Haussmann. The advances in building technology allowed the further development of theater building elements, such as extremely projecting tiers made of concrete (theater in Morges by François Hennebique, 1899). Modern theater construction frequently aimed to integrate the stage more into the auditorium, in line with the original Greek theaters, such as the Totaltheater by Walter Gropius (1926) and the organic designs of Friedrich Kiesler. Or they attempted to break through the strict frontal design such as the Liederhalle in Stuttgart as the first asymmetrical concert hall designed by Rolf Gutbrod and Adolf Abel.

PROJECTS.

MUMUTH – HAUS FÜR MUSIK UND MUSIK-THEATER DER KUNSTUNIVERSITÄT GRAZ,
GRAZ, AUSTRIA

UNSTUDIO

www.unstudio.com

Type: Music theater, **Setting:** Inner city, **Client:** BIG Bundesimmobiliengesellschaft m.b.H., Universität für Musik und darstellende Kunst Graz (KUG), **Completion:** 2009, **Number of auditoria:** 1, **Number of seats:** 450, **Additional functions:** Venue and rooms for practicing, **Photos:** UNStudio © / Iwan Baan (10, 14, 15), UNStudio © / Christian Richters (12/13).

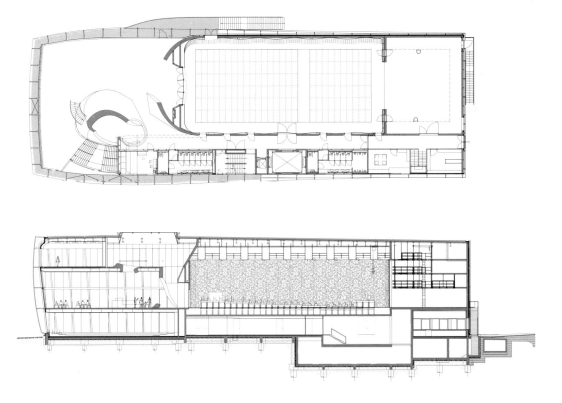

Left: Stairways in the foyer. | Right: Floor plan first floor, longitudinal section.

The architecture of this building clearly communicates that this is a place where music lives. Two main themes dominate the construction: The first one is the so-called 'spring structure' which bears a direct relationship to music. As the organizing element, the spiral offers structure to the volumes that make up the theater, auditorium, rehearsal and utility spaces. The spiral splits into many smaller interconnected spirals that take on a vertical and a diagonal direction. This is the second theme which creates a free and fluent internal spatial arrangement, and is an important design model, named by the architects as 'blob-to-box'.

Glass façade, illuminated at night.

From left to right, from above to below:
Orchestra pit, stage,
auditorium and foyer.
Right: Façade.

HELMUT-LIST-HALLE,
GRAZ, AUSTRIA

ARCHITEKT MARKUS PERNTHALER

www.pernthaler.at

Type: Multifunctional venue, **Setting:** Inner city, **Client:** Prof. Dr. h. c. Dipl. Ing. Helmut List, AVL List GmbH Graz, **Completion:** 2002, **Number of auditoria:** 1, **Number of seats:** 1,200, **Additional functions:** Ball room, **Photos:** Paul Ott, Graz.

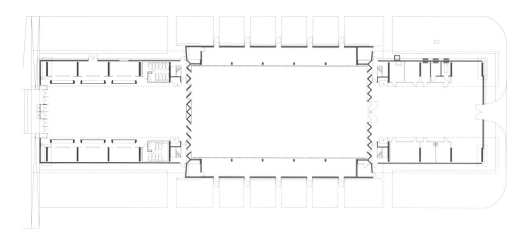

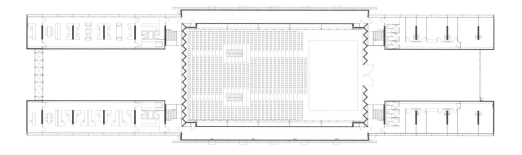

Left: Exterior. | Right: Ground floor plan and first floor plan.

One of the country's best concert halls was created from an industrial complex undergoing demolition. The building's natural oscillation, activated by frequencies conducted by the near-lying train tracks, were neutralized through innovative technical installations. An orchestra of dark-stained pine and monumentally folded end walls, together with individually adjustable ceiling elements and large-format steel weaves allow acoustic fine tuning. The outer structure is characterized by modern technical infrastructure which, in tandem with the roof construction of the former industrial hall, refers to the structure's industrial past.

Foyer

From left to right, from above to below:
Auditorium, main façade, detail solar
pannels on the façade, auditorium.
Right: Event space.

FRANZ LISZT CONCERT HALL,
RAIDING, AUSTRIA

ATELIER KEMPE THILL
ARCHITECTS AND PLANNERS

www.atelierkempethill.com

Type: Chamber music hall, **Setting:** Rural, **Planning partners:** Brands United / Grabner Ziviltechniker KEG für Architektur, Graz, **Client:** Franz-Liszt-Gesellschaft Burgenland, **Completion:** 2006, **Number of auditoria:** 1, **Number of seats:** 600, **Photos:** © Schwarz | Architekturfotografie.

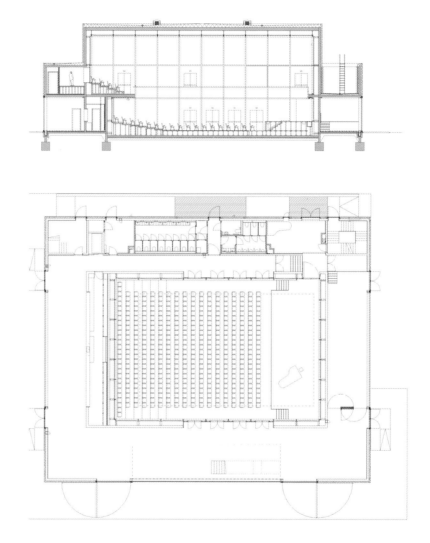

Left: Façade. | Right: Longitudinal section, ground floor plan.

The new concert hall is designed to extend the existing spatial context. Like the surrounding structures, it is enclosed by white walls and has windows just at the ground floor. The ambition of the design is to maintain the intimate atmosphere of the nearby park and realize an organic relationship between the interior and the surrounding landscape. The public foyer is hereby the key spatial element. All functions are placed inside a two-story volume which encloses the music hall. Inside, the space is dominated by white walls and a wooden floor. The façade is dramatically opened up on all sides using large, symmetrically positioned windows offering a spectacular view of the park.

From left to right, from above to below:
Façade, foyer, courtyard, stairways.
Right: Auditorium.

MUSIKVEREIN EXTENSION,
VIENNA, AUSTRIA

HOLZBAUER AND PARTNER, WILHELM HOLZBAUER, DIETER IRRESBERGER

www.holzbauer.com, www.holzbauer-partner.at

Kind: Concert, Setting: Inner city, Original building: Theophil Hansen, 1870, Client: Gesellschaft der Musikfreunde Wien, Completion: 2004, Number of auditoria: 4, Number of seats: All: 630, main auditorium: 380, Photos: Stefan Olah.

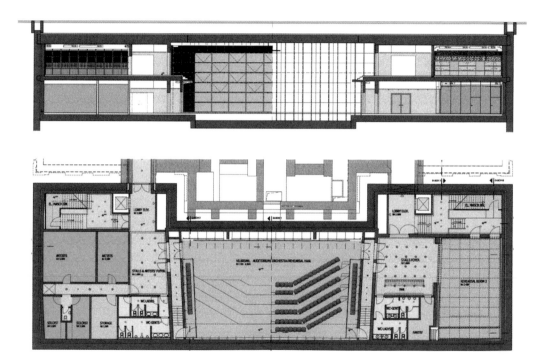

Left: The glass hall "Magna auditorium". | Right: Section and 3rd basement level.

The new addition of four halls underneath the square in front of the large hall of the Musikverein building incorporated a restructuring of the flow of visitors as well as the addition of cloak rooms, snacking and toilet facilities to the lounge areas. The new section was created immediately underneath the entrance lounge of the historical building. New stairways and elevators now connect all floors, allowing the highest degree of flexibility in the use of the existing and new halls. Special attention was paid to creating attractive and impressive elevator portals and vestibules. The invitingly light-flooded spaces allow visitors to forget the basement setting, while reflecting the surfaces of the old building through the use of terrazzo and plaster areas without stylistic replications.

From left to right, from above to below:
The glass hall "Magna auditorium",
the wooden hall, the stone hall.
Right: The metal hall.

NATIONAL CENTER FOR
THE PERFORMING ARTS,
BEIJING, CHINA

PAUL ANDREU ARCHITECTE PARIS

www.paul-andreu.com

Type: Theater, opera, ballet, **Setting:** Urban, **Planning partners:** ADPi and BIAD, **Client:** The Grand National Theater Committee, **Completion:** 1999, **Number of auditoria:** 3, **Number of seats:** Opera: 2,416, concert hall: 2,017, theater: 1,040, **Additional functions:** Art and exhibition spaces, **Photos:** Paul Maurer.

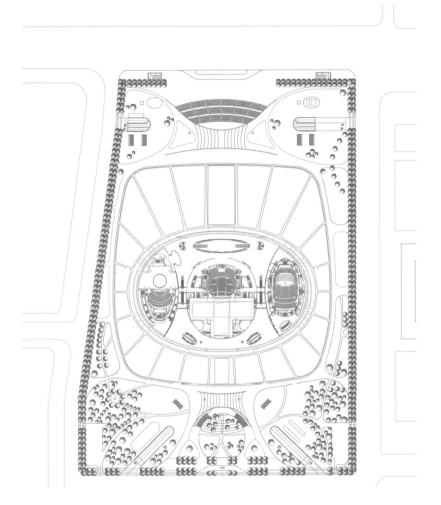

Left: Main entrance. | Right: Ground floor plan.

The National Grand Theater is a cultural island in the middle of a lake in the heart of Beijing, next to the Great Hall of the People. A titanium ellipsoid shell spans above the auditorium, measuring a maximum of 213 and a minimum of 144 meters. It is divided in two by a curved slab of glass which is 100 square meters wide at the base and 46 meters high. A 60-meter long transparent underpass connects it to the shore, leaving the exterior form intact. The public areas inside take the form of an urban district with streets, plazas, shopping areas, restaurants, quiet spaces and waiting lounges, with the opera house at the center and concert hall and theater flanking it on either side. The whole project can be described as a play on envelopes that succeed each other.

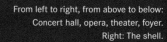

From left to right, from above to below:
Concert hall, opera, theater, foyer.
Right: The shell.

GUANGZHOU OPERA HOUSE,
GUANGZHOU, CHINA

ZAHA HADID ARCHITECTS

www.zaha-hadid.com

Type: Opera, **Setting:** Urban, **Client:** Guangzhou Municipal Government, **Completion:** 2010, **Number of auditoria:** 1, **Number of seats:** 1,800, **Additional functions:** Multifunction hall, auxiliary facilities & support premises, **Renderings and photos:** Courtesy of Zaha Hadid Architects.

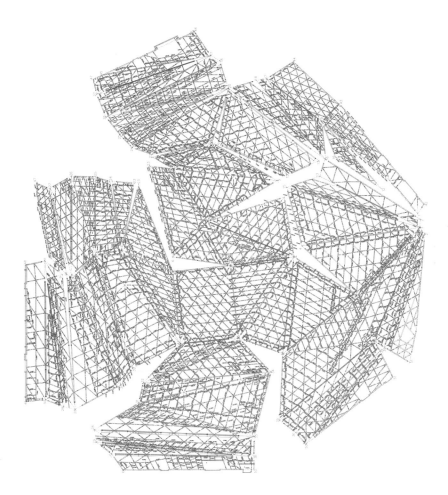

Left: Lobby. | Right: Structure (unfolded layout).

The Opera house, at the heart of Guangzhou's cultural sites development, adopts state-of-the-art technology in its design and construction. The structure rises and falls at the foot of Zhujiang Boulevard, bringing together two adjacent sites for the proposed museum and metropolitan functions. As an adjunct to the Haixinsha Tourist Park Island, the Opera House presents a contoured profile to provide a large riverside focus to visitors. An approach promenade, created as an internal street, cuts into the landscape beginning at the proposed museum site at the opposite side of the central boulevard and leads to the opera house. Cafe, bar, restaurant and retail facilities, embedded shell-like into these landforms, are located to one side of the approach promenade.

From left to right, from above to below:
Façade during construction
July 2009, lobby, stairs in the lobby,
façade during construction July 2009.
Right: Exterior view by night.

ZHUHAI OPERA HOUSE,
ZHUHAI, CHINA

SPF:ARCHITECTS

www.spfa.com

Type: Opera, **Setting:** Urban, **Client:** City of Zhuhai, **Completion:** ongoing, **Number of auditoria:** 1, **Number of seats:** 1,500, **Additional functions:** Rehearsal hall, restaurants, **Renderings:** Studio Pali Fekete architects (SPF:a).

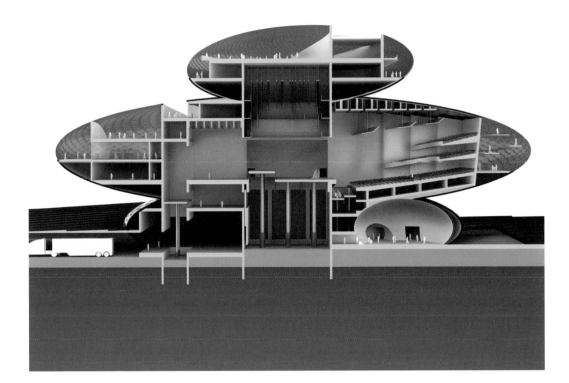

Left: Façade. | Right: Section.

The opera house in Guangdong Province is located on a man-made island just off the coast, giving it a striking visibility with the potential to become a landmark symbol of the city itself. SPF:a reconfigured an existing port into a backbone of retail and entertainment amenities. The concept reflects the originality and vibrant heart of the local culture in its elemental simplicity. The primary element of the scheme, a critical geographic and cultural element of Zhuhai, is a stone. The concept develops as a stack of rocks based on the principal of balance from the Five Element Theory (Earth, Wood, Fire, Metal, Water), a traditional Chinese philosophy. Site and opera house merge into poetic form, representing balance, function, and ecological harmony.

From left to right, from above to below:
The opera house behind the forest,
the Plaza of Fire, bird's-eye view Yeli Island.
Right: Interior view.

ROYAL PLAYHOUSE,
COPENHAGEN, DENMARK

LUNDGAARD & TRANBERG
ARKITEKTER

www.ltarkitekter.dk

Type: Theater, **Setting:** Inner city, **Client:** Danish Ministry of Culture, **Completion:** 2008, **Number of auditoria:** 3, **Number of seats:** All: 1,000, main auditorium: 650, **Photos:** Adam Mørk.

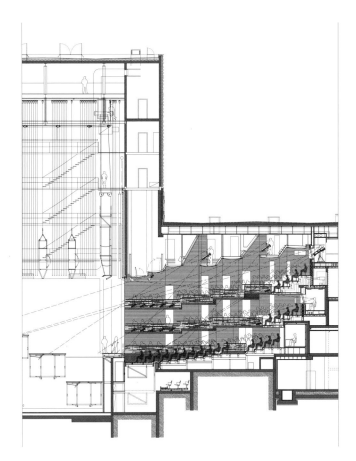

Left: Exterior by night. | Right: Section.

Firmly rooted in the context of its historic neighborhood, the playhouse takes its place among the culture institutions along the harbor. The building consists of three clear compositional elements: a powerful brick core with scene and auditorium, a promenade over the water with a glass foyer open to the public, and a projecting upper service level clad in green glass with varying nuances. At the heart of the playhouse is a circular, grotto-like auditorium, constructed of striking, staggered masonry walls that provide impeccable acoustics necessary for the unique meeting of the public with the theatrical spectacle. The theater contains a large auditorium with 650 seats, a port auditorium with 250 seats, and a small auditorium with 100 seats.

From left to right, from above to below:
Exterior by night, sea front, foyer, seating area.
Right: Main auditorium.

PERFORMERS HOUSE FOLK HIGH SCHOOL,

SILKEBORG, DENMARK

SCHMIDT HAMMER LASSEN
ARCHITECTS

http://shl.dk

Type: Theater, dance, music, education, **Setting:** Urban, **Client:** Performers House, **Completion:** 2007, **Number of auditoria:** 1, **Number of seats:** 400, **Additional functions:** Institute of performing art, **Photos:** Courtesy of schmidt hammer lassen architects.

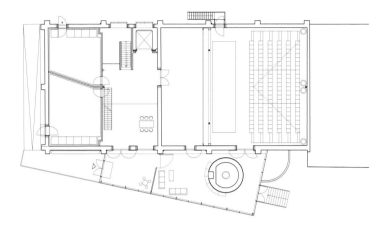

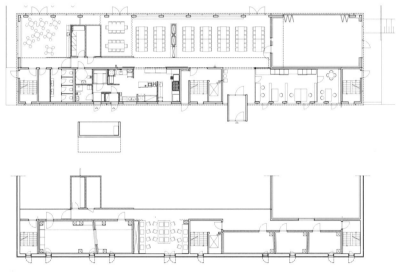

Left: Façade detail. | Right: Ground floor old boiler building and ground floor new building.

Performers House, situated at the heart of the Paper Mill's revitalized industrial area, is a modern interpretation of an institute of performing art. The old heating plant has been transformed into a winter garden, with an instruction room and a performance area, while an adjacent plaza links the historic building with its modern counterpart. The architectural style and choice of materials are simple and bold, expressing the area's industrial heritage. The demarcation between interior and exterior and between the individual elements in the academy organism are continually redrawn, making it possible for passersby to hear music or catch a glimpse of theatrical performances.

From left to right, from above to below:
Façade new building, interior, foyer, old building
reflected in the window of the new building.
Right: New building at night.

LE QUAI,
ANGERS, FRANCE

www.architecture-studio.fr

Type: Theater, **Setting:** Urban, **Client:** City of Angers, **Completion:** 2007, **Number of auditoria:** 5, **Number of seats:** All: 1,570, main auditorium: 970, **Additional functions:** Dancing school (CNDC), restaurant, **Photos:** Luc Boegly.

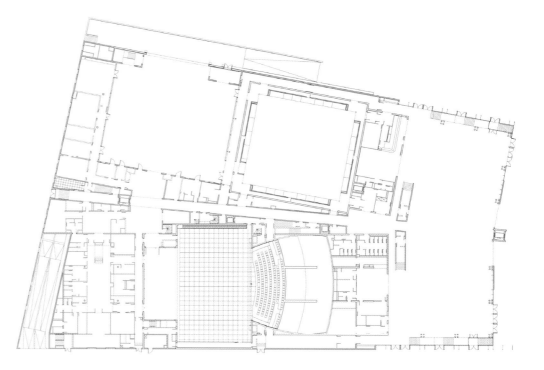

Left: Exterior view from Le Maine river. | Right: Ground floor plan.

The theater is a major project for both the town and the region. Developed around the trend of "creation, training and urban animation", the theater's architecture enhances urban character and strengthens the link between town, performance areas and dance school. Le Quai theater is a location where live shows are created and three rhythms, each with specific requirements, co-evolve. The rhythm of performance needs preserved and autonomous venues; the rhythm of audience is aided by venues that are integrated with the urban space; and finally, the rhythm of the dancing school, which requires specific educational spaces. The town and the theater were linked using a peristyle open onto the town, framing magnificent views on the King René Castle.

View onto the forum.

From left to right, from above to below:
Inner façade of the forum,
façade, forum at night.
Right: Main autidorium.

LE PRISME,
AURILLAC, FRANCE

BRISAC GONZALEZ ARCHITECTS

www.brisacgonzalez.com

Type: Concert hall**, Setting:** Urban**, Client:** Municipality of Agglomeration du Bassin d'Aurillac**, Completion:** 2007**, Number of auditoria:** 1**, Number of seats:** 2,500**, Additional functions:** Exhibitions, fairs, sport, **Photos:** Thierry Bonnet (54), bga/London (56 a.), Hélène Binet (56 b., 57).

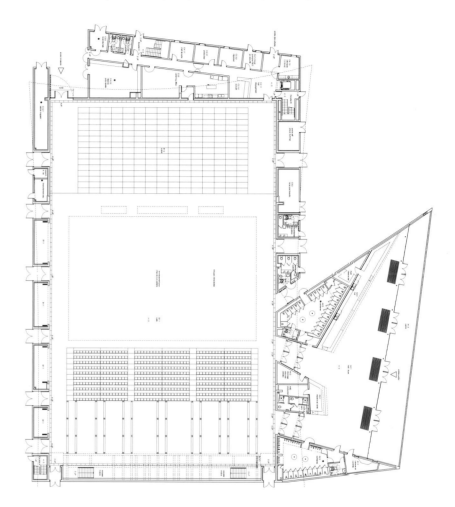

Left: Façade. | Right: Ground floor plan.

The new venue for concerts, theater, trade fairs and sport events is located on the outskirts of the city center, adjacent to the main train station. Due to the fact that the venue has no permanent residents, the building is essentially a chamber for ephemeral events. The main event space accommodates up to 4,300 people and contains retractable seating and a de-mountable stage for versatility. During the day, sunlight shines on 25,000 custom-built glass bricks with a pyramid shape which are embedded in the façade, producing shimmering effects and dramatic shadows. At nightfall, the building awakens as the Fresnel lens-like brick surfaces amplify the intensity of the controlled colored lighting scheme, producing a glittering solitaire set in the landscape.

From left to right, from above to below:
Night view, foyer, adaptable event hall.
Right: Entrance hall.

DIJON PERFORMING ARTS CENTER,
DIJON, FRANCE

ARQUITECTONICA

www.arquitectonica.com

Type: Theater, opera, ballet, symphony, **Setting:** Inner city, **Interior design:** Arquitectonica Interiors, **Client:** City of Dijon, **Completion:** 1998, **Number of auditoria:** 2, **Number of seats:** 2,240, **Photos:** Paul Maurer, Paris (58, 8 a. l., 60 a. r., 60 b. r., 61), Eric Morrill, Paris (60 b. l.).

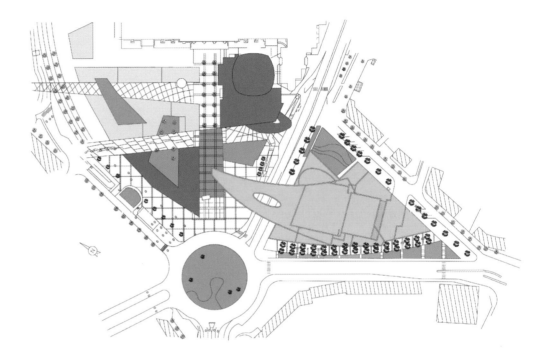

Left: View looking north-east. | Right: Site plan.

The Dijon Performing Arts Center includes a 1,640-seat symphony hall / performing arts center and a 600-seat conference center in Dijon. The main building is a state-of-the-art symphony hall and opera house that was the second structure to be completed as part of Arquitectonica's master plan for a new urban district. The composition of modern structures is crisscrossed by pedestrian walkways that lead to boldly-shaped exterior courtyards carved out of the solid mega-block. The new center bridges over the boulevard, acting as a gateway from the modern city to the historic district. The elevated lobby crosses the street, linking the building to the glass-enclosed galleria and the entrance to the exposition halls.

From left to right, from above to below:
Reception, main stage,
reception escalators, main stage seating.
Right: View looking north.

LIMOGES CONCERT HALL,
LIMOGES, FRANCE

www.tschumi.com

Type: Concert hall, **Setting:** Suburban, **Site architect:** ArchitectAtelier 4, **Landscape architect:** Michel Desvigne with Sol Paysage, **Client:** Community of Limoges, **Completion:** 2007, **Number of auditoria:** 1, **Number of seats:** 6,000, **Additional functions:** Administrative and concert production rooms, **Photos:** Peter Mauss/ESTO (62, 64 a. r., 64 b.), Christian Richters (64 a. l., 65).

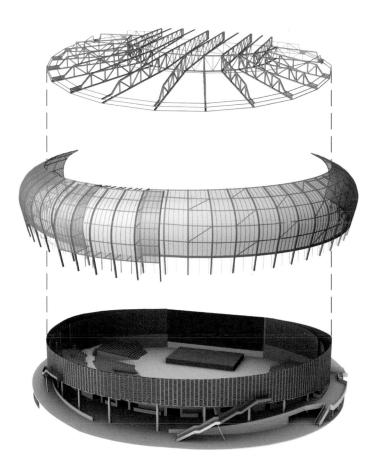

Left: Façade. | Right: Structural composite.

The outer envelope of the concert hall is made of wood arcs and translucent rigid polycarbonate sheets. The inner envelope consists of wood, whose use was suggested by the hall's location within a large forest. The configuration of the double envelope with interstitial circulation is a scheme that is advantageous for both acoustic and thermal reasons. Two ramps, one extending down, toward the lower tiers of the auditorium, and the other reaching upward to the upper tiers act as movement vectors between the two envelopes. Natural ventilation is integrated into the concept to keep the climate of the foyer at a temperate level, requiring little additional heating.

From left to right, from above to below:
Façade, ambulatory, ramps.
Right: Exterior by night.

PHILHARMONIC HALL,
PARIS, FRANCE

www.jeannouvel.com

Type: Philharmonic hall, **Setting:** Urban, **Planning partners concert hall:** Métra et Associés, **Light artist:** Yann Kersalé, **Client:** La Philharmonie de Paris, **Completion:** 2012, **Number of auditoria:** 1, **Number of seats:** 2,400, **Photos:** artefactory (66, 68 a., 68 b. r.), Ateliers Jean Nouvel (67, 69), Gaston & Septet (68 b. l.).

Left: Auditorium. | Right: Concept scheme auditorium.

The Paris philharmonic, known up until now for its opera houses, is to be erected at the Parc de la Villette, next to the Tschumis Cité de la Musique and the Conservatory according to plans that were drafted in 1995. The first concert hall to be built in the city since 1927 will fit 2,400 guests and is designed on the outside as an aluminum clad mound with an area of 20,000 square meters, which provides a view of the northeastern Arrondissement. To limit the distance of any guest to less than 100 meters from the stage, the building was created according to a "vineyard" concept. Suspended balconies also allow the sound to reach the listeners from behind.

From left to right, from above to below:
View from Porte de Pantin, detail, balconies.
Right: Exterior view.

CONCERT HALL & EXHIBITION COMPLEX,
ROUEN, FRANCE

BERNARD TSCHUMI ARCHITECTS

www.tschumi.com

Type: Concert hall, **Setting:** Suburban, **Client:** District of Rouen, **Completion:** 2001, **Number of auditoria:** 1, **Number of seats:** 7,000, **Additional functions:** Exhibition hall, **Photos:** Peter Mauss/Esto (70, 72 a. l., 72 b. l., 73) Bernard Tschumi (72 a. r., 72 b. r.).

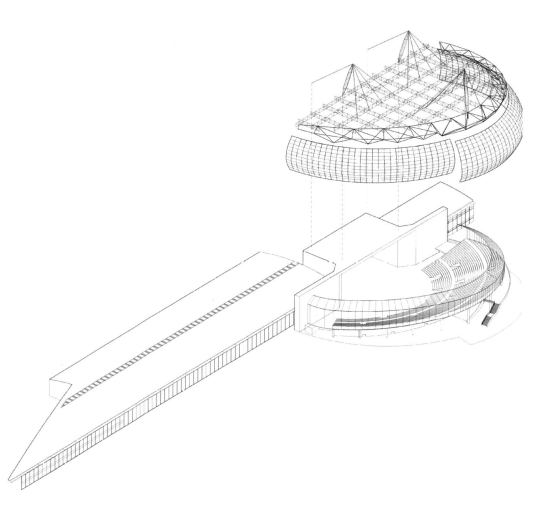

Left: Exterior view by night. | Right: Axonometry.

The project was initiated as a civic tool capable of simultaneously fostering economic expansion and cultural development of the district and provides a strong contemporary image on the town's outskirts. The concert hall accommodates musical as well as sporting events, political conventions, and theatrical shows. The classic concert hall typology has been transformed with a slight asymmetry in the audience seating which lends spontaneity to pop music and other media evens while permitting the theater to be reconfigured into three smaller volumes. Acoustical concerns led to a complete double envelope surrounding the concert hall. The entry lobby is located between the two skins.

From left to right, from above to below:
Seats in the auditorium, foyer, stairs
in the foyer, foyer.
Right: Façade.

ZENITH MUSIC VENUE,
SAINT-ETIENNE, FRANCE

FOSTER + PARTNERS

www.fosterandpartners.com

Type: Concert hall, **Setting:** Suburban, **Planning partners:** Cabinet Berger, **Artist:** Guillermo Quintero (mesmerising stage curtain), **Client:** City of Saint-Etienne, **Completion:** 2008, **Number of auditoria:** 1, **Number of seats:** 1,100 to 7,200, **Photos:** Nigel Young / Foster + Partners.

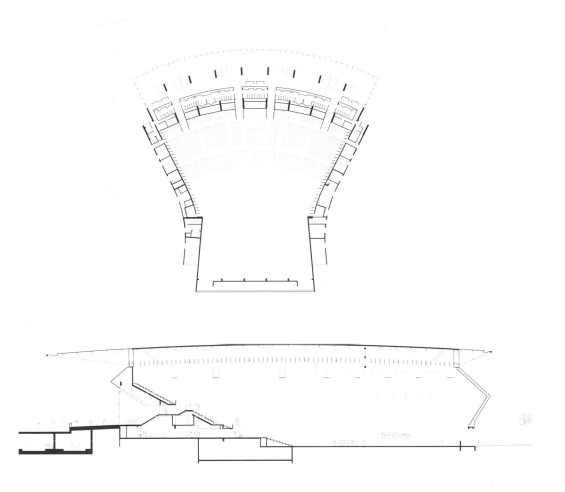

Left: Front. | Right: Floor plan and section.

The Zénith is a state-of-the-art music and cultural facility for St. Etienne which places the former industrial city on the cultural map, forming the heart of an exciting project aimed to revitalize the area to the northeast of the city center. On the outside, it is characterized by a large, cantilevered roof which utilizes the valley winds to assist natural ventilation and cooling. A broad ramp provides access to the glazed foyer which spans across a busy road and houses the artists' and backstage facilities. The plazas in front of the building and the foyer are shaded by a deep overhang of the roof canopy. Inside, the venue offers flexible performance space and auditoriums which can be configured for capacities that range from 1,100 to 7,200.

From left to right, from above to below:
Foyer, auditorium, roof.
Right: Canopy.

ZENITH STRASBOURG,

STRASBOURG, FRANCE

STUDIO FUKSAS

www.fuksas.it

Type: Music hall, **Setting:** Suburban, **Client:** City of Strasbourg, **Completion:** 2008, **Number of auditoria:** 1, **Number of seats:** 10,000, **Photos:** Aidiasol (78), Moreno Maggi (80 a. l., 80 a. r.), Philippe Ruault (81).

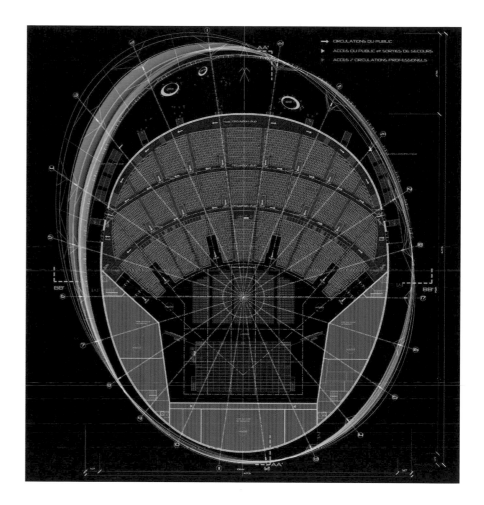

Left: Bird's-eye view. | Right: General plan.

With its playful form and character, the Zenith music hall contributes to the great varietè theaters which have been built after the Zenith building in Paris was erected in 1984. It is the new attraction of the city's exhibition area, giving a new impulse to the development of Strasburg's infrastructure. The building is to be understood as a single, unifying and autonomous sculpture. By layering and rotating the ellipsoid metal façade structure, the design receives a very dynamic character. This is underlined using the translucent textile membrane which covers the steel frame and creates magnificent light effects. This building balances good views for all spectators, great acoustics and an optimized cost management.

From left to right, from above to below:
Bridge, façade, auditorium.
Right: Foyer.

KOMISCHE OPER BERLIN,
BERLIN, GERMANY

STEPHAN BRAUNFELS
ARCHITEKTEN BDA

www.braunfels-architekten.de

Type: Music theater, **Setting:** Inner city, **Original building:** Büro Fellner & Helmer, 1892, **Client:** Stiftung Komische Oper Berlin, **Completion:** 2007, 2010, **Number of auditoria:** 1, **Number of seats:** 1,273, **Photos:** Ulrich Schwarz, Berlin.

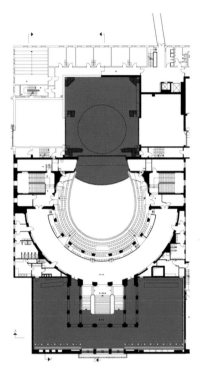

Left: Stairways. | Right: Floor plan.

While the auditorium and the neo-Baroque staircase of the opera house survived the ravages of WWII without significant damage, the reconstructed foyers, cloakrooms, bars, ticket offices and the concert stage had to undergo a redesign. Following the latest renovation, the room-height mirrored façade finish reflects the neo-Baroque ambulatories of the stairwell from new angles. The anthracite-colored, dampened mirrors also act to extend it into infinity. Seating benches with leather upholstery stretch along the walls. Spherical lights were left in place. Foyer floors and the bar areas are executed in red, like the ceilings and counters of the cloakroom, continuing a color accent derived from the color of the theater's logo.

Foyer.

From left to right, from above to below:
Foyer, stage, booking office.
Right: Cloakroom.

BOCHUM CONCERT HALL,
BOCHUM, GERMANY

VAN DEN VALENTYN ARCHITEKTUR

www.vandenvalentyn.de

Type: Concert hall, **Setting:** Inner city, **Client:** City of Bochum, **Completion:** –, **Number of auditoria:** 1, **Number of seats:** 1,200, **Additional functions:** Café, administration, **Photos:** Van den Valentyn Architektur, Cologne.

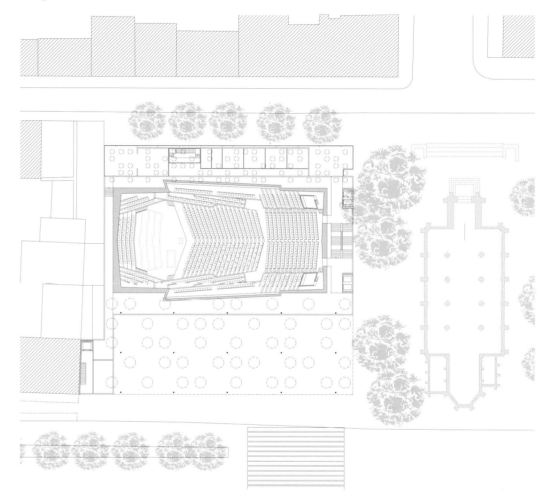

Left: Perspective auditiorium. | Right: Floor plan third floor.

The symphony completes the structure of the city block to the south and is optically delimited to the north by the Church of our Lady. Two streets with contrasting character crisscross the area. A roofed-over urban space shaped like a loggia acts as a generous reception for concertgoers. A semi-transparent, semi-translucent roof, whose edges continue the city block development, shelters the loggia, foyer, concert hall and the artists' and administrative areas. Towards the church, the building appears as a low-key solitary volume. Inside, the visitor is presented with exciting spatial and communications solutions which delta in the lively concert hall at a respectful distance to the musicians.

From left to right, from above to below:
Elevation Victoriastraße,
elevation Humboldstraße,
elevation Marienplatz.
Right: Perspective Victoriastraße.

BEETHOVEN FESTIVAL THEATER,
BONN, GERMANY

VAN DEN VALENTYN ARCHITEKTUR

www.vandenvalentyn.de

Type: Festival theater, **Setting:** Urban, **Client:** Deutsche Post AG, Bonn, **Completion:** –, **Number of auditoria:** 2, **Number of seats:** All: 2,000, main auditorium: 1,500, **Additional functions:** Restaurant, Beethoven-Café, shop, sky-bar, multipurpose hall, outdoor performance space, **Photos:** Van den Valentyn Architektur, Cologne.

Left: Perspective small auditorium. | Right: Floor plan auditorium and foyers.

The new Bethoveen Hall cultural complex combines world-class architecture and top-notch acoustics in a strict urban design. The area consisting of four large quadrants is to be rearranged in order to offer maximum integration of culture and city life. The design places each quadrant (a tree-lined parking lot, an open lawn, the concert hall itself, as well as the Rhine and embankment setting around the hall) in the context of the cautiously developing European city. The successful recent history of Bonn's urban development receives a new chapter with these expressive, individual architectures, rooted in part in the quadrant.

From left to right, from above to below:
South elevation from Theaterstraße,
perspective Rhine terrace,
east elevation Rhine bank.
Right: Perspective large auditorium.

STAGES OF THE CITY OF COLOGNE,
COLOGNE, GERMANY

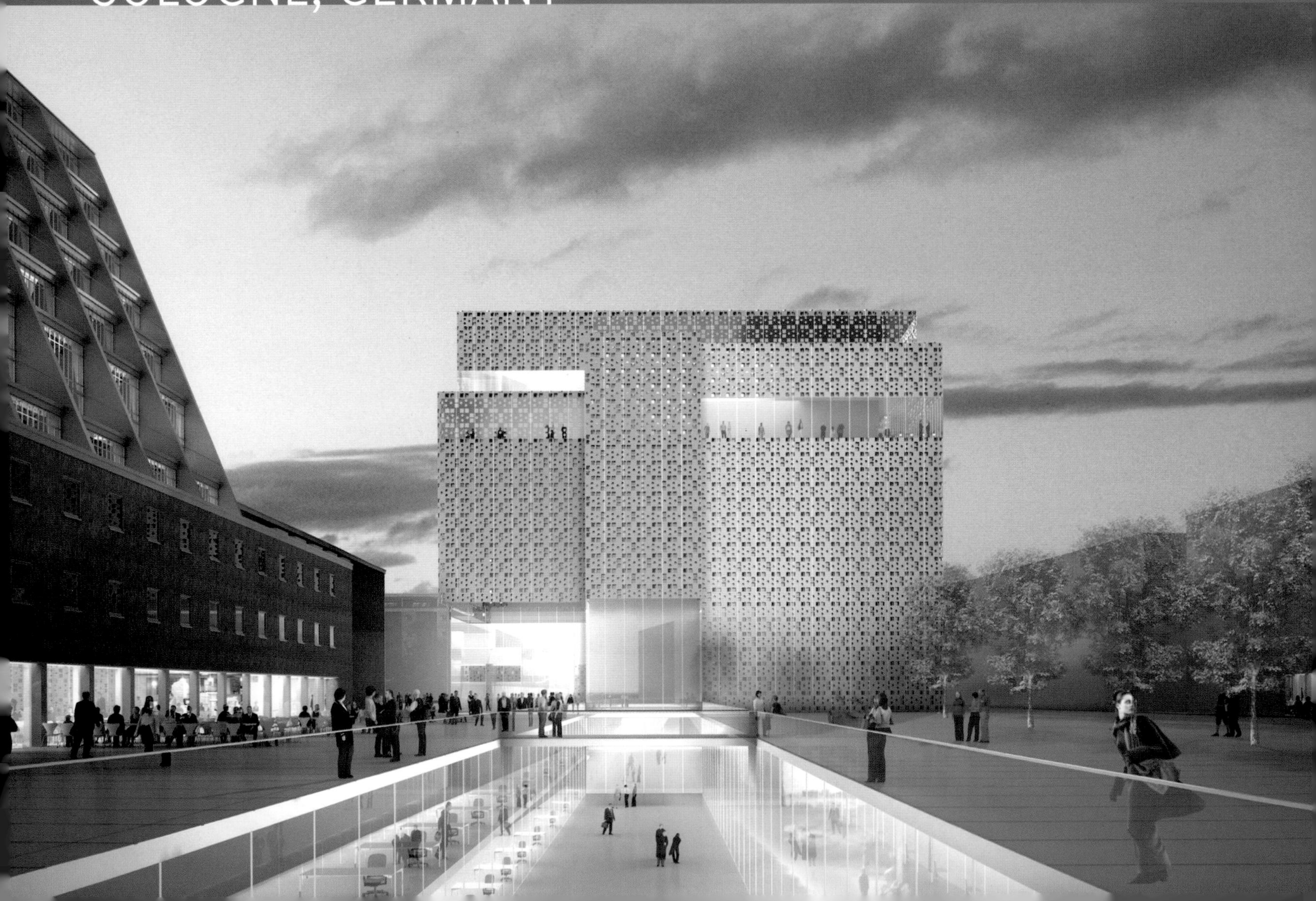

JSWD ARCHITEKTEN
CHAIX & MOREL ET ASSOCIÉS

www.jswd-architekten.de

Type: Theater, opera, **Setting:** Inner city, **Original building:** Wilhelm Riphahn, 1957 (opera), 1962 (theater), **Client:** Bühnen der Stadt Köln, **Completion:** 2013, **Number of auditoria:** 2, **Number of seats:** All: 2,450, main auditorium: 1,350, **Additional functions:** Children's opera, **Renderings and photos:** JSWD Architekten / Chaix & Morel et associés (96–98), Christoph Seelbach, Köln (99).

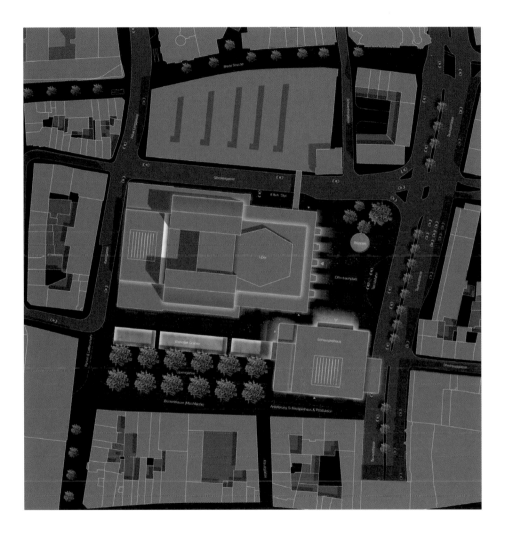

Left: Perspective Operngarten. | Right: Site plan.

Together with the listed opera house by Wilhelm Riphahn, the new theater creates an ensemble of equal partners. The compact solitary body of the new building and the opera house, freed of all adjoining buildings, create two high-quality urban spaces. The newly framed Offenbach Square is reaffirmed as an urban forum and a representative space. The theater is organized in a tower-like fashion – the stages are stacked one on top of the other inside the compact building. This creates complex spatial successions with alternating vertical and horizontal sightlines. The visitor's path from the street level through the main foyer and continuing to the halls (main hall, rehearsal stage, restaurant) is not just a prelude, but is part of the theatrical experience.

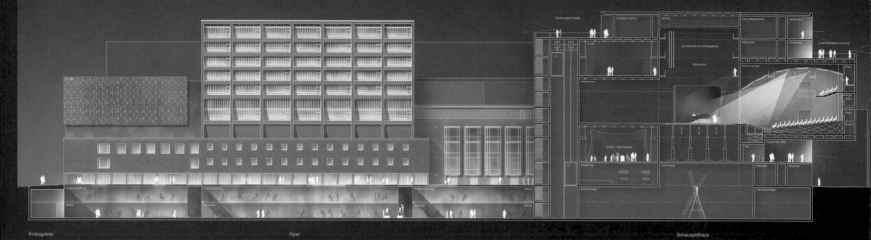

Kreuzgasse   Oper   Schauspielhaus

From above to below:
Section, perspective Offenbachplatz.
Right: Opera hall.

HESSISCHES STAATSTHEATER,
DARMSTADT, GERMANY

LEDERER+RAGNARSDÓTTIR+OEI

www.archlro.de

Type: Theater, opera, ballet, **Setting:** Inner city, **Planning partners:** DU Diederichs, Wuppertal (project management), **Original building:** Rolf Prange, 1972, **Client:** State of Hesse, **Completion:** 2006, **Number of auditoria:** 3, **Number of seats:** 956, **Photos:** © Roland Halbe / artur.

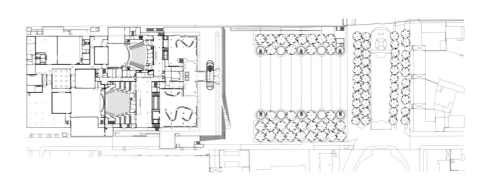

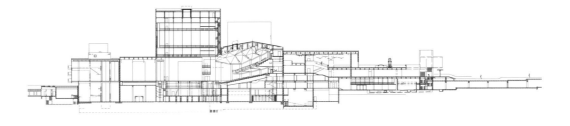

Left: Façade of the new entrance building. | Right: Ground floor plan and longitudinal section.

The functionality of this building, erected in 1972 as one of Germany's largest post-war theaters, remains exemplary to this day. However, like many structures of the time, the theater was precariously integrated into the urban plan and spatial situation of the site and appeared very closed-off with its below-ground driveway and internal stairwell. The new entrance volume acts as the theater's central access. It offers not just a new representative entry with a shielding canopy, but also an open air stage on the second floor, which opens onto the square. This way, the theater enters into a dialogue with its urban context in a straightforward way, relating to the neighboring church and obelisk.

From left to right, from above to below:
Box office, bar level, stairways.
Right: Ondulated façade of the new entrance building.

RESTRUCTURING PALACE OF CULTURE,
DRESDEN, GERMANY

GMP – VON GERKAN, MARG AND PARTNERS ARCHITECTS

www.gmp-architekten.de
Type: Concert hall, opera, cabaret, **Setting:** Inner city, **Planning partners:** Meinhard von Gerkan and Stephan Schütz with Nicolas Pomränke, **Original building:** Leopold Wiel, Wolfgang Hänsch, Herbert Löschau, 1969, **Client:** City of Dresden, **Completion:** 2014, **Number of auditoria:** 2, **Number of seats:** All: 2,150, main auditorium: 1,800, **Additional functions:** Library, restaurants, visitor center Frauenkirche, **Renderings:** gmp Architects.

Left: Auditorium. | Right: Situation.

The new concept for the hall and the integration of a central library aims to return the theater's original central role as an urban cultural meeting place. The unique central location between the old market, castle grounds and the new market requires the building to be open from all sides. The auditorium's design follows the wish for a centering, integrating and acoustically optimized organization of the orchestra. The original auditorium's hexagonal form and the centered position of the stage creates a vineyard-like audience seating placement. Individual terraces are displaced around the orchestra's "epicenter" like tectonic plates.

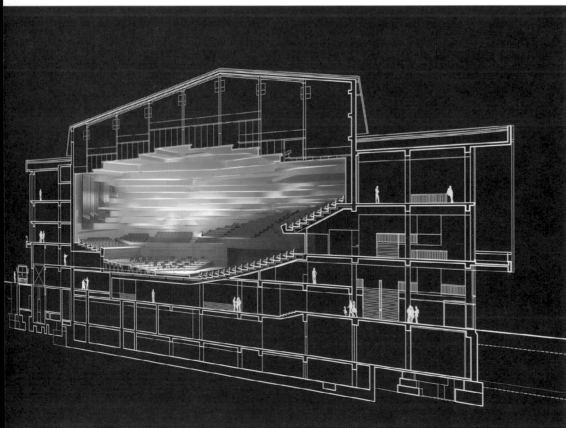

From left to right, from above to below:
Elevation Altmarkt, section, library.
Right: Cabaret "Herkuleskeule".

CARL MARIA VON WEBER COLLEGE OF MUSIC,
DRESDEN, GERMANY

HAMMESKRAUSE ARCHITEKTEN

www.hammeskrause.de

Type: Concert hall, **Setting:** Inner city, **Client:** SIB II Dresden, **Completion:** 2008, **Number of auditoria:** 1, **Number of seats:** 450, **Additional functions:** Stage for rehearsals, rooms for practicing, library, **Photos:** Stefan Müller-Naumann, Munich.

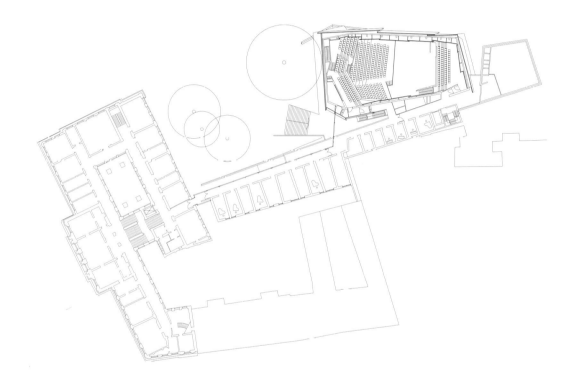

Left: Entrance area. | Right: Floor plan first floor.

The neo-Renaissance college building has been expanded with a new extension, which reveals the building's essence and purpose – music. The old and new buildings engage in a benevolent dialog as two substantial parties. The opera rehearsal stage and studios form a clear edge towards the city, and the concert hall stands in front as a solitary unit. Its en-velope dissolves on the exterior and on the interior and develops a unique, independent spatial concept. Slabs, panels and boards are closely packed around the auditorium and the musicians. This creates a high degree of authenticity in the structure's spatial impression, both inside and outside: the hall reveals itself as a counter-draft of the older building.

From left to right, from above to below:
Orchestra and balconies, ceiling, stage.
Right: Stage, orchestra and balconies.

**INTERIOR DESIGN
DEUTSCHE OPER AM RHEIN,**
DUSSELDORF, GERMANY

RKW ARCHITEKTUR + STÄDTEBAU

www.rkw-as.de

Type: Opera, **Setting:** Inner city, **Interior architects:** RKW Interior design, **Original building:** Ernst Giese, 1875, **Client:** Deutsche Oper am Rhein, **Completion:** 2009, **Number of auditoria:** 1, **Number of seats:** 1,342, **Additional functions:** Foyer, **Photos:** Stefan Müller.

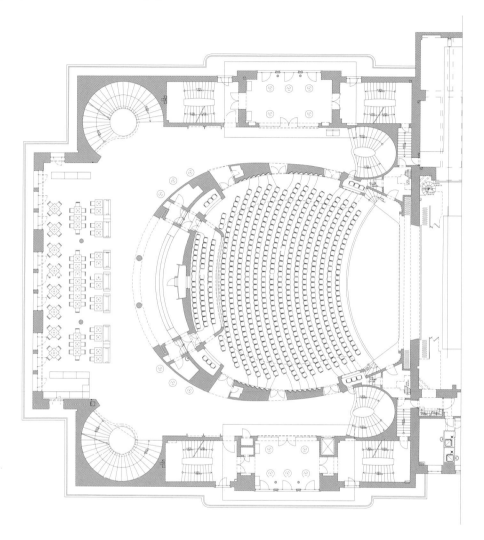

Left: Auditorium. | Right: Ground floor plan, foyer.

Constructed in neo-Renaissance style, the theater was renovated in the 1950s, and experienced a refurbishment and addition of a light-filled orchestra and a ballet rehearsal space in 2007. During the latest modernization of the complete foyer, new lounge furnishings, information/exhibition stands and catering areas were created. The tiers with VIP lounges and dining facilities are individually designed using not only layout, but also through varied furnishings, thereby creating various spatial effects with the help of carefully chosen materials. The elegant lines found in the architecture are continued in the building's appointments.

Cloak room.

From left to right, from above to below:
First balcony, information desk, foyer, desk.
Right: Stairways.

ACADEMY OF MUSIC AND THEATER CONCERT HALL "FELIX MENDELSSOHN BARTHOLDY"
LEIPZIG, GERMANY

GERBER ARCHITEKTEN

www.gerberarchitekten.com

Type: Concert hall, **Setting:** Inner city, **Artist:** Andrew Topolski, New York, **Interior design:** Hans-Christoph Bittner, **Original building:** Hugo Licht, 1885–1887, **Client:** State of Saxony, **Completion:** 2001, **Number of auditoria:** 1, **Number of seats:** 450, **Additional functions:** Event center, **Photos:** Courtesy of Gerber Architekten / Hans Jürgen Landes.

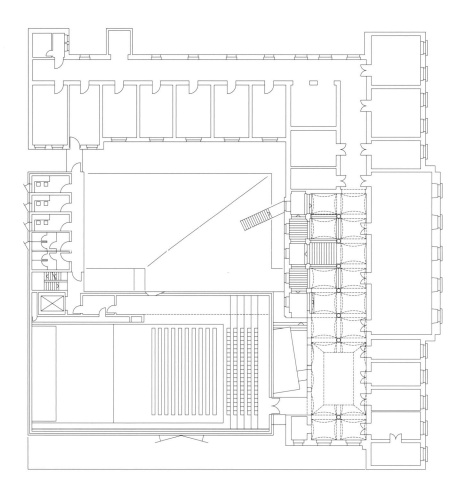

Left: Façade. | Right: Second floor plan.

The exterior of the new concert hall in the south wing is clad in wood and presents itself as a contemporary sculpture of an architectural sound space. On the west perimeter, a bar which rests on slim discs, also clad in wood, completes the building's corner. It wraps around the formerly unutilized yard and creates an outdoor concert space with a new set of characteristics. The corridors in the new west wing and the concert hall itself open toward the yard through the glass façade. This way, the yard presents the communicative, identity-forming heart of the music school, opening additional ways to experience it.

From left to right, from above to below:
Detail, auditorium, clad in wood,
passageway between new and old building.
Right: Stage.

HALLE MUENSTERLAND,
MUENSTER / WESTPHALIA, GERMANY

KRESING ARCHITEKTEN

www.kresing.de

Type: Congress center and event space, **Setting:** Urban, **Original building:** Felix Sittel, 1926, roof: 1948, **Client:** Messe und Congress Centrum Halle Münsterland GmbH, **Completion:** 2009, **Number of auditoria:** 2, **Number of seats:** 3,697, **Photos:** Sven Otte, Cologne.

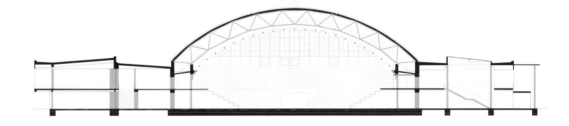

Left: Business lounge. | Right: Section.

The new concept for the traditional Halle Muensterland known far and wide outside the region transforms the multi-purpose venue into an event center with a special character. The program layout and spatial structure create a stage for various uses via several building blocks including the central auditorium and frontal halls and lounges. The creative implementation is not only functional, but itself takes on the role of an actor. Design elements draw a reaction from and interact with the audience, letting the space to become the stage itself in part. Sensible creativity and perfect direction perfectly complement each other.

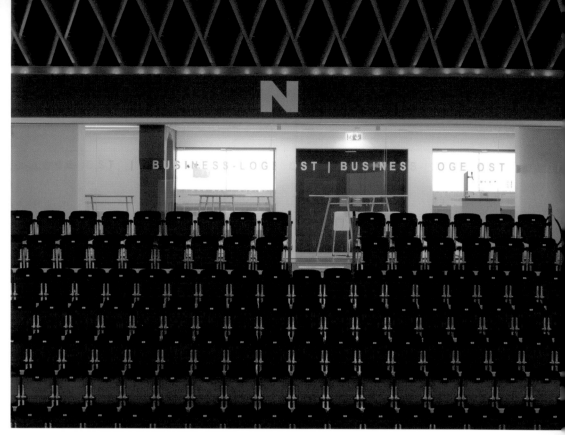

From left to right, from above to below:
Ladies room, business lounge, foyer, green room.
Right: Central hall.

NATURE THEATER AUDITORIUM,
REUTLINGEN, GERMANY

4A ARCHITEKTEN

www.4a-architekten.de

Type: Open-air theater, **Setting:** Suburban, **Client:** Naturtheater Reutlingen e.V., **Completion:** 2008, **Number of auditoria:** 1, **Number of seats:** 1,000, **Photos:** Patrick Beuchert, Wertheim.

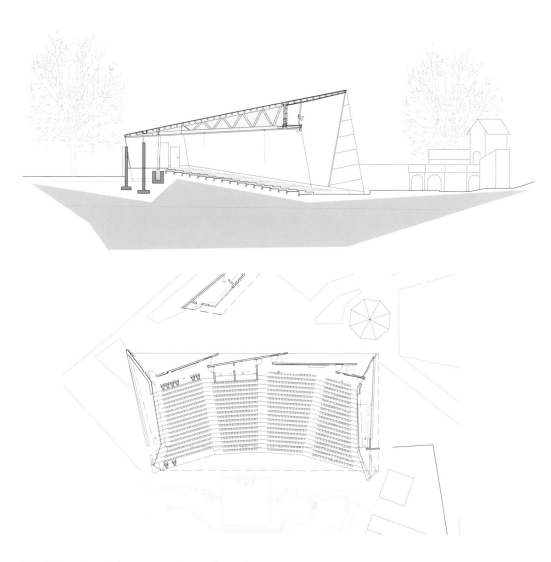

Left: View from the auditorium to the open-air stage. | Right: Section and floor plan.

The auditorium in the middle of the woods completely keeps with the client's wishes - "light, open and modern". The cantilevered, self-supporting roof structure shelters the 1000-seat auditorium and the foyer, which provides a protected space during bad weather. The green metal cladding integrates the building into its environment. Depending on the light conditions, the surrounding trees create varying dynamic reflections on the façade. The auditorium's interior is completely clad in wood. Narrow bands of light structure the ceiling and accent the form's dynamics.

From left to right, from above to below:
Foyer from auditorium, entrance,
façade from south-east, entrance area.
Right: Auditorium.

VISUAL – CENTRE FOR CONTEMPORARY ART & GEORGE BERNARD SHAW THEATRE,
CARLOW, IRELAND

www.terrypawson.com
Type: Theater, art gallery, **Setting:** Urban, **Client:** Carlow County Council, **Completion:** 2009, **Number of auditoria:** 1, **Number of seats:** 355, **Additional functions:** Exhibition spaces, café, **Photos:** Hélène Binet (130, 132/133, 134 a. l., 134 a. r.), Ros Kavanagh (134 b. l., 134 b. r., 135).

Left: North-east corner. | Right: Sketch interior.

The Visual provides Ireland with a significant new exhibition space to showcase contemporary visual arts and a theater of national and international importance. Set in the picturesque setting of the grounds of St. Patrick's College, it features an expansive gallery space for touring international contemporary exhibitions. The entrance, located on the south elevation, opens into a foyer of cast concrete and dark timber which leads up a short flight of stairs to the galleries or left to the George Bernard Shaw Theater located in the south-west corner of the building. It contrasts with the serene neutrality of the gallery spaces and is defined by a deep red feature wall in the foyer bar and red seating in the auditorium.

East elevation with raised planted promenade alongside the reeded pond.

From left to right, from above to below:
Main gallery with clerestory glazing, theater bar,
link gallery, east elevation at night showing link gallery.
Right: Entrance area at night.

WEXFORD OPERA HOUSE,
WEXFORD, IRELAND

OFFICE OF PUBLIC WORKS
IN IRELAND
WITH KEITH WILLIAMS ARCHITECTS

www.opw.ie, www.keithwilliamsarchitects.com

Type: Opera, **Setting:** Inner city, **Client:** Wexford Festival Opera, **Completion:** 2008, **Number of auditoria:** 2, **Number of seats:** 780, **Photos:** Ros Kavanagh, Ireland.

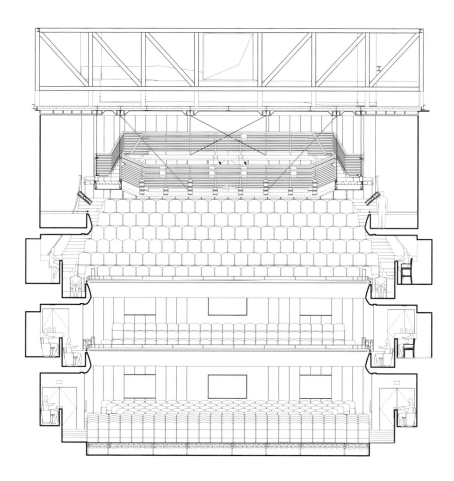

Left: Main auditorium. | Right: Auditorium cross detail section.

Wexford Festival Opera has played a central role in Ireland's cultural life as well as in the international world of opera and the arts since 1951. The rebuilding of Wexford Opera House is one of Ireland's most important cultural projects of recent times, and was completed for the 2008 autumn opera festival. A totally new opera house has been constructed in the town center on the site of the old Theater Royal, the demolished former home of the world famous opera festival. The purpose-designed opera house contains two theaters of differing scales. The principal auditorium accommodates 780 seats, while the new, adaptable auditorium with 175 seats provides space for performances in a variety of formats.

From left to right, from above to below:
View of the opera house at twilight, main auditorium,
main stairs and atrium.
Right: Second stage, Jerome Hynes Theater.

RENOVATION OF THE THEATRE ALLA SCALA,
MILAN, ITALY

STUDIO ARCHITETTO MARIO BOTTA

www.botta.ch

Type: Theater, **Setting:** Inner city, **Original building:** Giuseppe Piermarini, 1778, **Client:** City of Milan, **Completion:** 2004, **Number of auditoria:** 1, **Number of seats:** 2,030, **Photos:** Pino Musi, Milan.

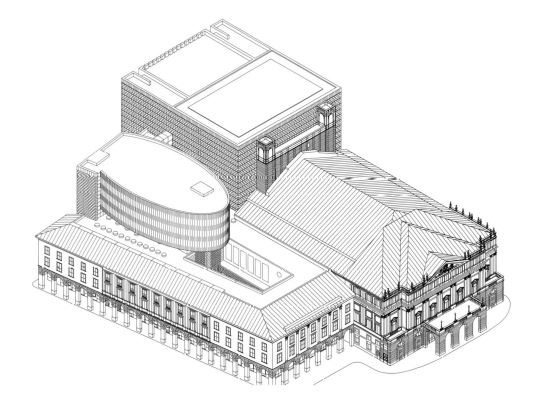

Left: Stage tower. | Right: Axonometry.

Intervention at the core of an historical city in order to adapt a highly symbolic building entails a risky cultural bet. Two volumes have been designed above the inner space of the pre-existing buildings: the stage tower volume, which strengthens the main axis of the Piermarini theater, and the elliptical volume, which constitutes an axis parallel to that of the theater. The order of the new volumes' axes underlines the various periods of the theater's development. The relationship between the historical sections and the new interventions mirrors the difficulties, but also the richness of this European city. The simultaneous presence of different influences is the sign of an intense background which confirms a social, civil and an aesthetic value to contemporary culture.

From left to right, from above to below:
Elliptical volume from the courtyard,
hall and stage, front view, courtyard.
Right: Nort-west façade.

143

ZA-KOENJI PUBLIC THEATER,
SUGINAMI-KU, TOKYO, JAPAN

TOYO ITO & ASSOCIATES

www.toyo-ito.co.jp

Type: Theater, **Setting:** Urban, **Client:** Suginami-ku, **Completion:** 2008, **Number of auditoria:** 3, **Number of seats:** 614, **Additional functions:** Café, **Photos:** Courtesy of Toyo Ito & Associates, Architects.

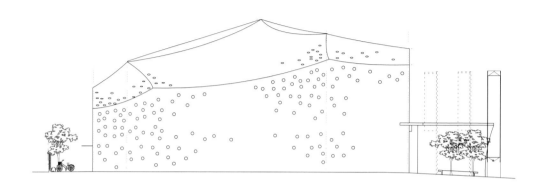

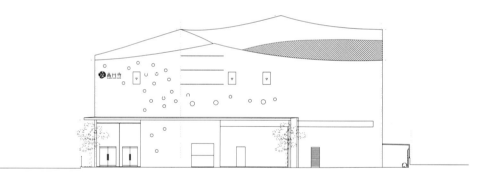

Left: West side. | Right: West and south elevation.

Replacing the old Koenji Hall, the theater is located within a residential district, five minutes' walking distance from the JR Koenji station in Tokyo. Taking into consideration the surrounding context and acoustic requirements of the building, a 'closed' space resembling a tent cabin with extremely thin walls and roof was built. The roof was carved out of a cube using five elliptic cones and two cylinders, resulting in a dynamic shape that expresses movement and lightness. The central axis, angles and coordinate positions of the elliptic cones and cylinders were defined as a result of negotiations between the height restrictions of the site and the height requirements of the internal programs.

From left to right, from above to below:
Stairs in the foyer, foyer,
main auditorium, entrance.
Right: View towards stage.

GIANT AMBER CONCERT HALL,
LIEPAJA, LATVIA

VOLKER GIENCKE & COMPANY

www.giencke.com

Type: Concert hall, **Setting:** Urban, **Client:** City of Liepaja, **Completion:** 2012, **Number of auditoria:** 2, **Number of seats:** 1,200, **Additional functions:** Business and event center, **Renderings and modell photos:** Giencke & Company/Graz.

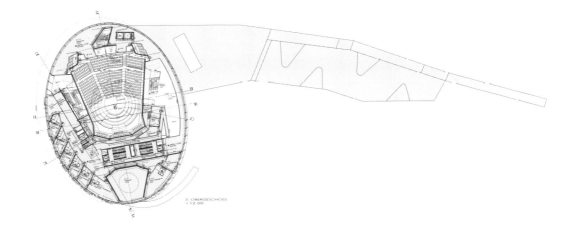

Left: Perspective. | Right: Ground floor plan.

The Giant Amber concert hall is not just a building, but a new indoor/outdoor location which transforms a square lying six meters above street level into a business and event center. The concert hall and the chamber music hall are the main musical functions. The lengthwise stretched commercial and event space, buckled in its top view, holds together and completes the uneven, slanted 35-meter high-glass concert hall cone. The square connecting both buildings is the primary entrance into the foyer. A street-level exhibition and performance area, named "Civita Nove" is to become the communal meeting point for Liepaja's population.

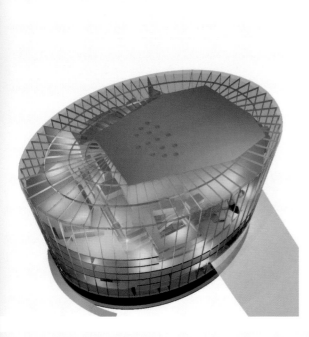

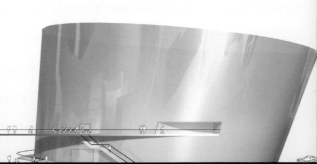

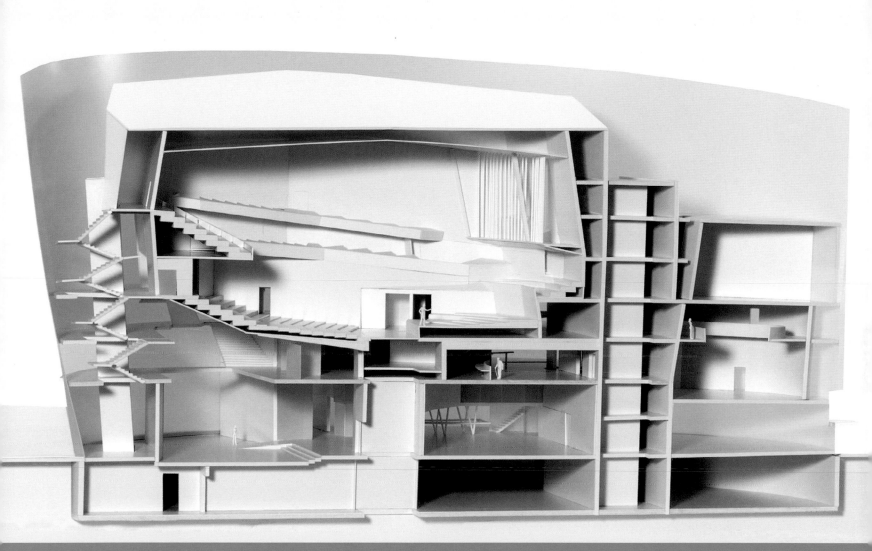

From left to right, from above to below:
Bird's-eye view, model, north elevation.
Right: Model photo section.

MIGDAL ARQUITECTOS /
JAIME VARON, ABRAHAM METTA,
ALEX METTA

www.migdal.com.mx

Type: Theater, opera, ballet, **Setting:** Urban, **Client:** Hidalgo government, **Completion:** 2005, **Number of auditoria:** 1, **Number of seats:** 2,000, **Photos:** Werner Huthmacher / Germany (152, 154 b.), Paul Czitrom / Mexico (154 a. l., 154 a. r., 155).

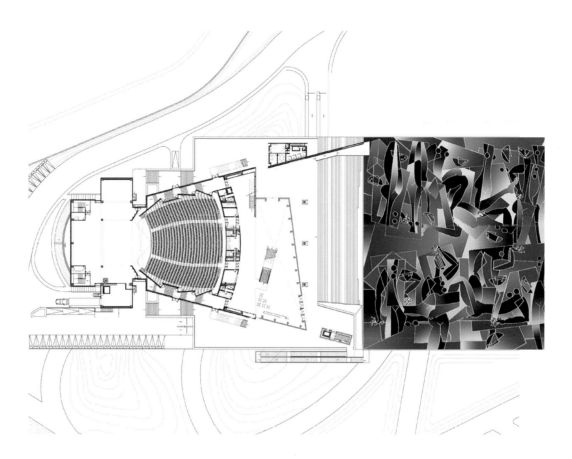

Left: Foyer. | Right: First floor plan.

The auditorium is situated at the southern tip of David Ben Gurion cultural and recreation park. It is positioned directly in front of a plaza with brightly colored mosaics that are reflected in the large surface of mirror glass mullions at the entrance to the auditorium. While the front of the building is mostly made up of huge glass windows, increasing transparency inside the foyer which provides a smooth transition into the auditorium, the back part of the building consists of a stone volume, housing the stage, backstage and theater machinery. Made up of concrete and steel, the outside is kept in black and silver tones, whereas red and brown colors were used inside in order to represent the project's vitality.

From left to right, from above to below:
Principal façade detail, main façade, concert hall.
Right: View to the mural plaza.

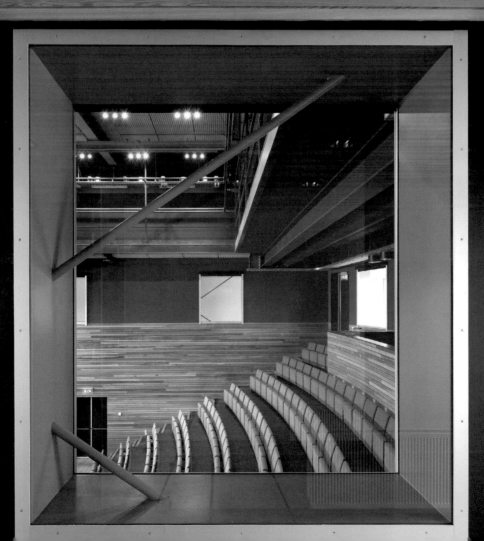

BIJLMER PARK THEATER,
AMSTERDAM, THE NETHERLANDS

ARCHITECTENBUREAU
PAUL DE RUITER BV

www.paulderuiter.nl

Type: Theater, circus, **Setting:** Urban, **Client:** City of Amsterdam, **Completion:** 2009, **Number of auditoria:** 1, **Number of seats:** 162 to 277, **Additional functions:** Youth theater school, studios, offices, **Photos:** Pieter Kers.

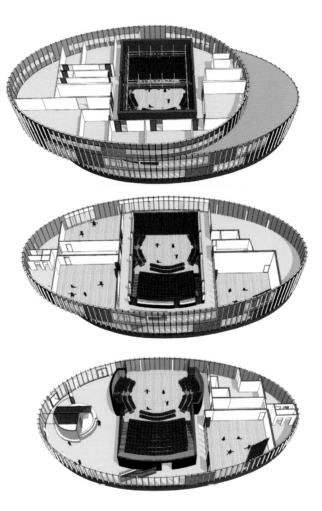

Left: View into the auditorium. | Right: Axonometry of the three floors.

The cultural building consists of an ellipsoid, with the upper two floors slightly displaced in relation to the ground floor. This creates a covered entrance area located in a logical position within the routing of the plan's urban development. The building's shape necessitated the search for a financially viable way of reproducing this rounded shape in the façade, partially of glass. The solution was found by pairing wooden slats and vertical aluminum strips against the steel-and-glass sections of the façade. As a result, the intersection points of the segmented façade are invisible, and the building exhibits a rounded, dynamic and somewhat abstract appearance which changes continuously as you walk around it.

From left to right, from above to below:
Foyer, exterior by night, at the first floor.
Right: Façade.

NEW AUDITORIUM STADSSCHOUWBURG,

AMSTERDAM, THE NETHERLANDS

JONKMAN KLINKHAMER
ARCHITECTUUR INTERIEUR
STEDENBOUW

www.jonkmanklinkhamer.nl

Type: Theater, ballet, popconcerts, **Setting:** Inner city, **Original building:** Van Gendt und Springer, **Client:** Stadsschouwburg, Melkweg, Toneelgroep Amsterdam, **Completion:** 2009, **Number of auditoria:** 2, **Number of seats:** 1,000, **Additional functions:** 2 rehearsal studio's, offices, workspaces, **Photos:** Christiaan de Bruijne, Koog aan de Zaan (160, 162, 163), Jonkman Klinkhamer, Amersfoort (161).

Left: Excisting Stadsschouwburg with the new auditorium at the background. | Right: Bird's-eye view.

The extension of the theater was designed as a volume set high above the existing Melkweg theater. The new auditorium rises 13 meters above street level, side by side with the 19th century stage of the old theater, separated by a 1.5 m wide gap. The complete back stage wall is made out of glass so that the audience can feel the new building's connection with the old structure. Characteristic of the extension is the foyer, which practically floats high above the city, and the innovative use of materials. The wooden stage floor is also repeated in the public areas of the new theater, and the interior finish of the walls and ceilings refers to the façade.

From left to right, from above to below:
Public space around the auditorium, foyer,
auditorium with on both sides the technical
galleries, luminous bench under the auditorium.
Right: Auditorium seen through the
louvres of the technical gallerie.

CONSERVATORIUM OF AMSTERDAM,
AMSTERDAM, THE NETHERLANDS

www.cie.nl

Type: Concert halls, **Setting:** Inner city, **Client:** Stichting Amsterdamse Hogeschool voor de Kunsten,
Completion: 2008, **Number of auditoria:** 5, **Number of seats:** 770, **Additional functions:** College building, study building, foyer with canteen, library, lecture hall, offices, **Photos:** Daria Scagliola & Stijn Brakkee.

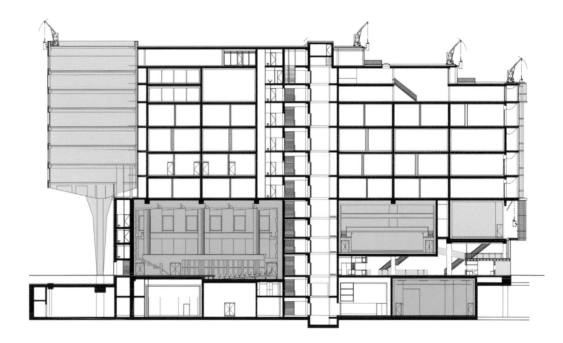

Left: Main auditorium "Bernard Haitinkzaal". | Right: Longitudinal section.

Plot 5 of Oosterdok island is part of a high-urbaniza-
tion project on the edge of the inner city, within the
former harbor area. The Amsterdam School of Music
has three parts: the 'performance center', consisting
of five auditoria for different types of performances
and the foyer annex canteen; the school building
with classrooms; and the study building with study
rooms, library, a lecture hall and offices. The design
follows this partitioning by organizing the vertical components into three clusters, ranging from
collective to individual, and from extraverted to
introverted. The building's order also means that it
is arranged around the school's most important aim:
music performance.

From left to right, from above to below:
Façade, auditorium "Sweelinckzaal",
auditorium "Blue Note", bird's-eye view.
Right: Engawa.

DELAMAR,
AMSTERDAM, THE NETHERLANDS

ACCA – JO COENEN AND ARNO MEIJS, AMA GROUP

www.jocoenen.com, www.ama-group.info
Type: Theater, plays, musicals, **Setting:** Inner city, **Client:** VandenEnde Foundation, **Completion:** 2010,
Number of auditoria: 2, **Number of seats:** 1,553, **Renderings:** AMA, Arno Meijs architects.

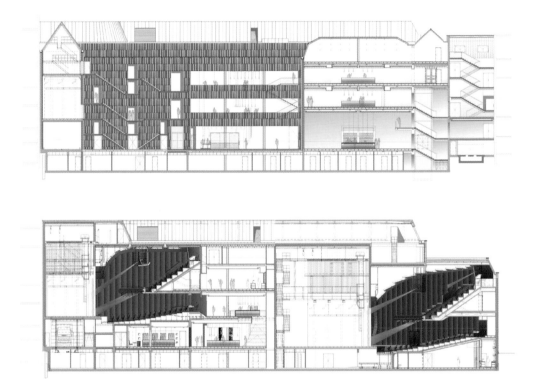

Left: Façade. | Right: Elevation and section.

Located on a traditional theater stretch, the DeLaMar replaces an outdated cinema and the old "Nieuwe de la Mar" theater. While the 1950s cinema will be demolished, the neo-Renaissance buildings to either side of it will be partially preserved and partially reconstructed, helping integrate the new glass volume into the urban fabric. Constitut- ing a part of an arching perimeter development with a complex layout, the building includes a re- hearsal space and two theater halls. The interior of the new structure presents an interplay of modern- ism and traditional theater atmosphere, and aims to provide continuity to the renowned theater and cabaret program.

From left to right, from above to below:
Foyer auditorium 1, bar, auditorium 2 during rehearsal, foyer.
Right: Balcony auditorium 1.

MUZIEKGEBOUW,
AMSTERDAM, THE NETHERLANDS

www.3xn.dk

Type: Music hall, **Setting:** Inner city, **Client:** City of Amsterdam, **Completion:** 2005, **Number of auditoria:** 1, **Number of seats:** 800, **Additional functions:** Jazz club, **Photos:** Adam Mørk, Copenhagen.

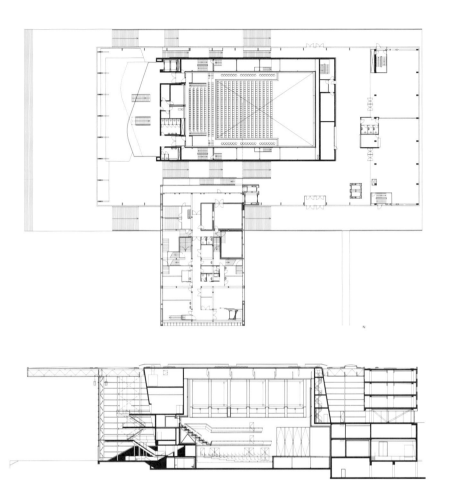

Left: Exterior at dusk. | Right: Second floor plan and section.

The center for modern music and jazz is positioned at the tip of the Oosterlijke Handelskade pier, close to the heart of the old canal city. Providing new common premises for two well-established institutions, the Ijsbreker and the BIMhuis, the building has become a magnet for a sophisticated music audience as well as for public activity, while acting as a landmark facing the fjord IJ. It is a truly public, democratic building, designed for an open, 24/7 flow. Wide staircases connect to the pier and waterfront and act as a spectacular access route to the interior. The café, documentation center, exhibitions and audio playground are some of the features open to the public. Large glass façades let in a flood of filtered, soft daylight.

Concert hall.

From left to right, from above to below:
Open floors, balconies, concert hall.
Right: Waterfront at dusk.

POPSTAGE MEZZ BREDA,
BREDA, THE NETHERLANDS

ERICK VAN EGERAAT

www.erickvanegeraat.com

Type: Pop stage, **Setting:** Inner city, **Client:** Municipality of Breda, **Completion:** 2002, **Number of auditoria:** 1, **Number of seats:** 650, **Additional functions:** Bar and café, **Photos:** Christian Richters.

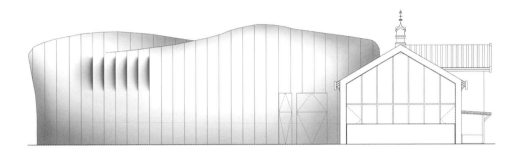

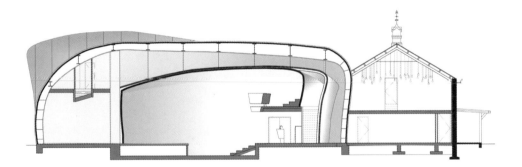

Left: Entrance. | Right: South façade and section.

As part of the urban development scheme by OMA for the abandoned military campus Chassée in Breda, a former officers' mess hall dating from 1899 will be converted into a venue for Breda's pop music fans. The extension accommodating the concert hall and foyer is shaped like a voluptuous sea shell adjoining the existing structure. In order to meet the strict acoustic requirements for pop concerts, the shell is formed as a complete double dome. The outer shell is rotated in relation to, and it's shape determined by the inner shell. The outer shell support is a hybrid structure of steel and concrete which is covered by 100 mm of pouring concrete and a pre-oxidated copper skin for acoustic reasons.

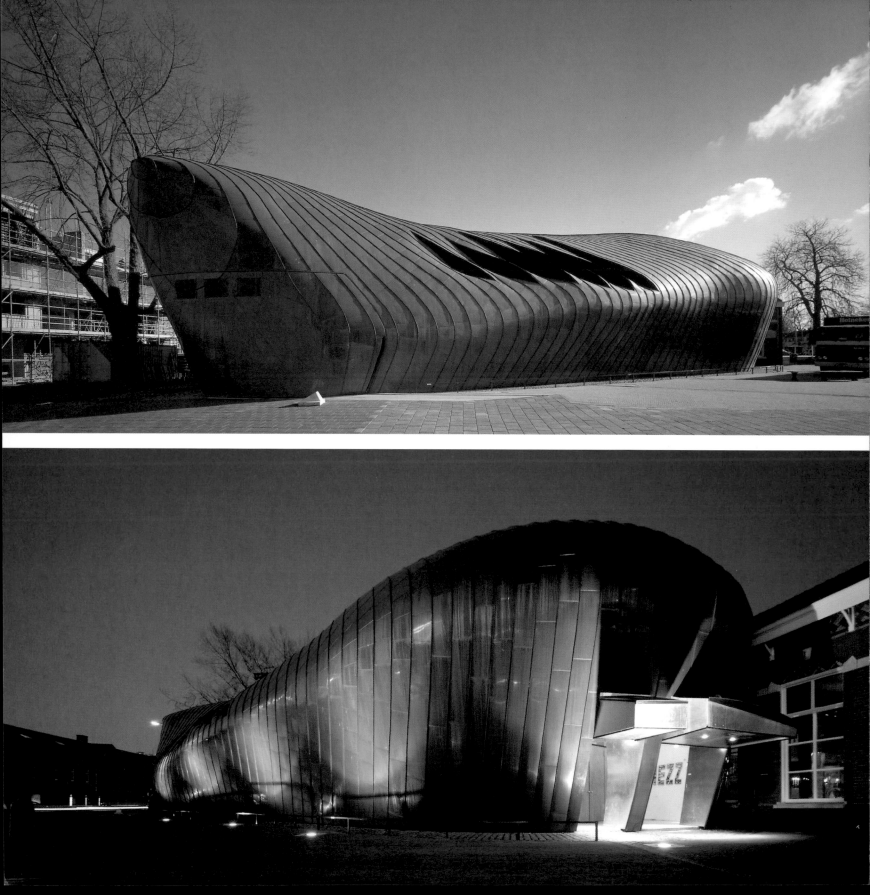

From left to right, from above to below:
Exterior view, south façade.
Right: Stage.

SCHOUWBURG AMPHION,

DOETINCHEM, THE NETHERLANDS

MECANOO ARCHITECTEN

www.mecanoo.nl

Type: Theater, **Setting:** Inner city, **Client:** Cultureel Centrum Schouwburg Amphion N.V., Doetinchem, **Completion:** 2010 **Number of auditoria:** 2, **Number of seats:** Great hall: 870, small hall: 300, **Additional functions:** Theater café, **Renderings:** Mecanoo architecten.

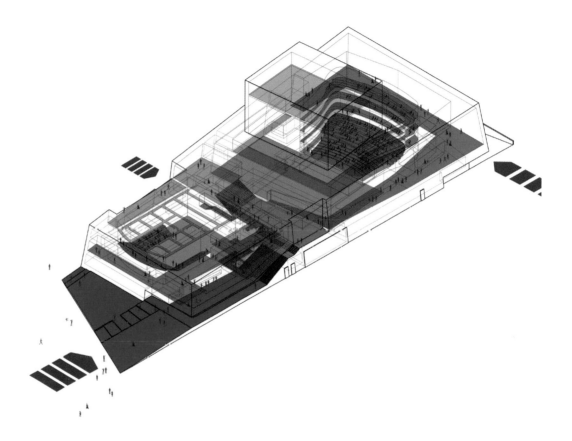

Left: Entrance. | Right: Axonometry.

Schouwburg Amphion was a popular theater in the center of the Dutch city Doetinchem, but could not keep up with modern day demands. In a new neighborhood to the northeast of the city center and close to the shops, cafés and restaurants, the new building with a fluent transition from exterior to the interior will provide a special theatrical experience for visitors in its own right. Like a red carpet, the entry ramp invites passersby inside. Through the entrance hall and via the grand staircase, visitors are led to the foyer around the two theater halls. The halls have distinct interiors and an atmosphere that differs from the foyers: the large auditorium is reminiscent of traditional 18th and 19th century theaters, while the small references the former Amphion.

From left to right, from above to below:
Main auditorium, model, section.
Right: Gateway.

PHILHARMONIC ORCHESTRA
AND CONCERT HALL,
HAARLEM, THE NETHERLANDS

DE ARCHITEKTEN CIE. / FRITS VAN DONGEN

www.cie.nl

Type: Concert halls, **Setting:** Inner city, **Designer glass façade:** Karel Martens, **Original building:** A. van der Steur, 1878, **Client:** Municipality of Haarlem, **Completion:** 2005, **Number of auditoria:** 2, **Number of seats:** All: 1,645, main auditorium: 1,230, **Additional functions:** 3 music salons, **Photos:** Daria Scagliola & Stijn Brakkee, Allard van der Hoek, Rob Hoekstra.

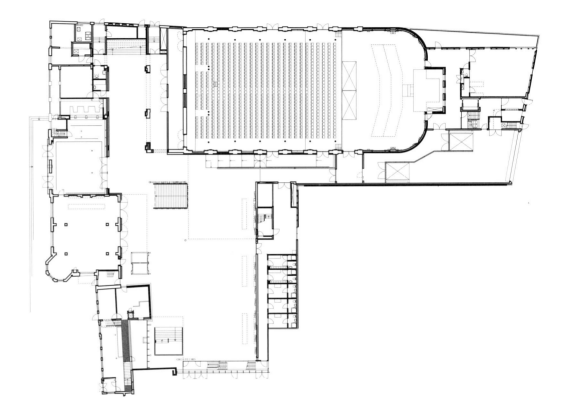

Left: Foyer behind the original building. | Right: Ground floor plan.

The building, which was constructed as an association building, but served as a concert hall starting from the early 20th century, has undergone a radical metamorphosis. In addition to a thorough renovation and restoration of the existing structure, it has also received an extension, executed in a manner that achieves perfect harmony between the old and new parts. The fully-fledged music center with five auditoria has a clear-cut and logical layout. The main hall has been extended, the stage has been enlarged, the balconies have been joined into one continuous whole, and the classic ceilings and detailing were restored. The new small concert hall is a suspended structure that appears to float in the foyer.

From left to right, from above to below:
In the foyer, bird's-eye view,
small concert hal, main auditorium.
Right: Glazed façade adorned
with a design by Karel Martens.

CITY THEATER HAARLEM,
HAARLEM, THE NETHERLANDS

ERICK VAN EGERAAT

www.erickvanegeraat.com

Type: Theater, **Setting:** Inner city, **Artist:** Babs Haenen (design ceramic ornaments), **Client:** Municipality of Haarlem, **Completion:** 2008, **Number of auditoria:** 1, **Number of seats:** 658, **Photos:** Christian Richters.

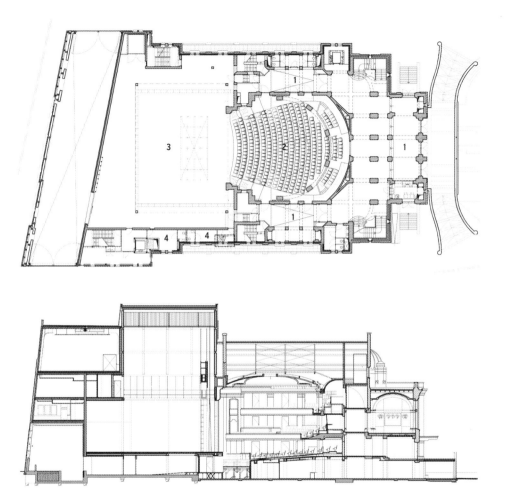

Left: Entrance. | Right: Ground floor plan and section.

The cultural landmark in the historic city center dating from World War II is a listed monument. The existing theater no longer met contemporary theater technique, production facility and building accessibility requirements. The new design included renovation, careful restoration and extension of the existing theater. The most striking intervention to the monument is the replacement of the original flight tower by a new, expanded structure. The visual impact of this extension is minimized through the cascading layering of the façade, letting it dissolve into the air. Brickwork, ornamented porcelain and partially screen-printed glass are integrated into the existing eclectic Art Deco façade.

Exterior view.

From left to right, from above to below:
Foyer, auditorium, bar, auditorium detail.
Right: Corridor.

195

POP PODIUM DE VORSTIN,

HILVERSUM, THE NETHERLANDS

www.cie.nl

Type: Tagrijn pop podium, **Setting:** Inner city, **Client:** City of Hilversum, **Completion:** 2009, **Number of auditoria:** 1, **Number of seats:** Auditorium: 700, music café: 300, **Additional functions:** rehearsal rooms, **Photos:** Courtesy of de Architekten Cie.

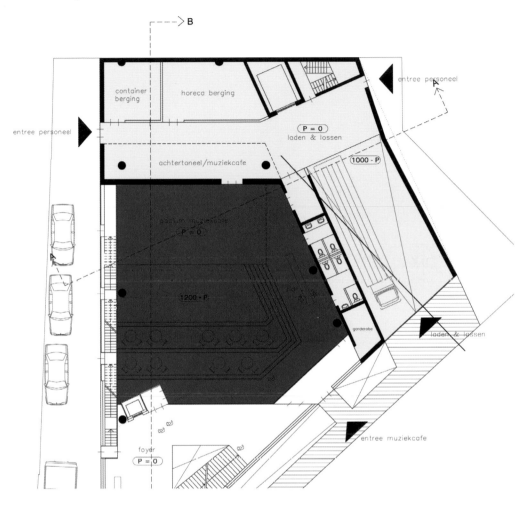

Left: Exterior. | Right: Floor plan entrance hall.

The Tagrijn pop stage is situated at a prominent location within walking distance from the railway station, at a major crossroad in the inner city. The building's façade with the entrance and foyer act as the visiting card to the Koninginneweg bank. Two main functions determine the structure: the main auditorium with a closed character and the music café with a more open ambience. The passageways and the auxiliary function as a buffer around the two auditoria, thus efficiently realizing soundproofing for the environment. This layout simultaneously generates the pop stage's image: the spatial and architectonic representation of the new pop stage is fashioned according to the 'box within a box' principle.

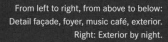

From left to right, from above to below:
Detail façade, foyer, music café, exterior.
Right: Exterior by night.

THEATER AGORA,
LELYSTAD, THE NETHERLANDS

UNSTUDIO

www.unstudio.com

Type: Theater, **Setting:** Urban, **Client:** City of Lelystad, **Completion:** 2007, **Number of auditoria:** 2, **Number of seats:** 960, **Additional functions:** Congress center, **Photos:** UNStudio © / Iwan Baan (200, 202), Christian Richters (203).

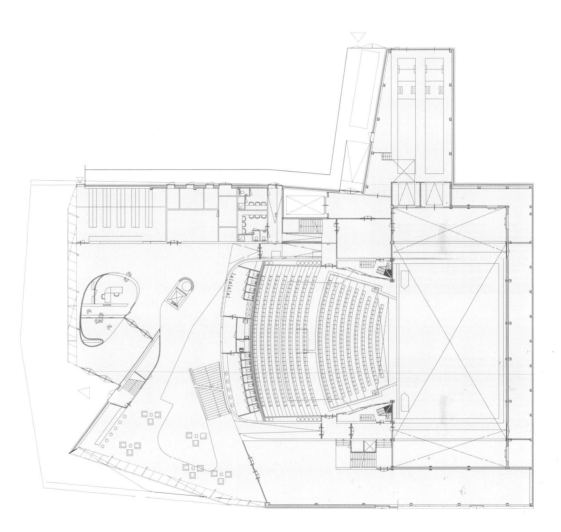

Left: Main theater. | Right: Ground floor plan.

The Agora theater projects an extremely colorful and upbeat character. A handrail executed as a snaking pink band cascades down the main staircase, winds itself around the void at the center of the large, open foyer space and then extends up the wall toward the roof. The main theater is executed completely in red and features a spacious stage, accommodating large international productions. The façades have sharp angles and jutting planes covered by steel plates and glass, which often overlap and come in shades of yellow and orange. These protrusions afford spaces where the spectacle continues off-stage, and the roles of performer and viewer may be reversed.

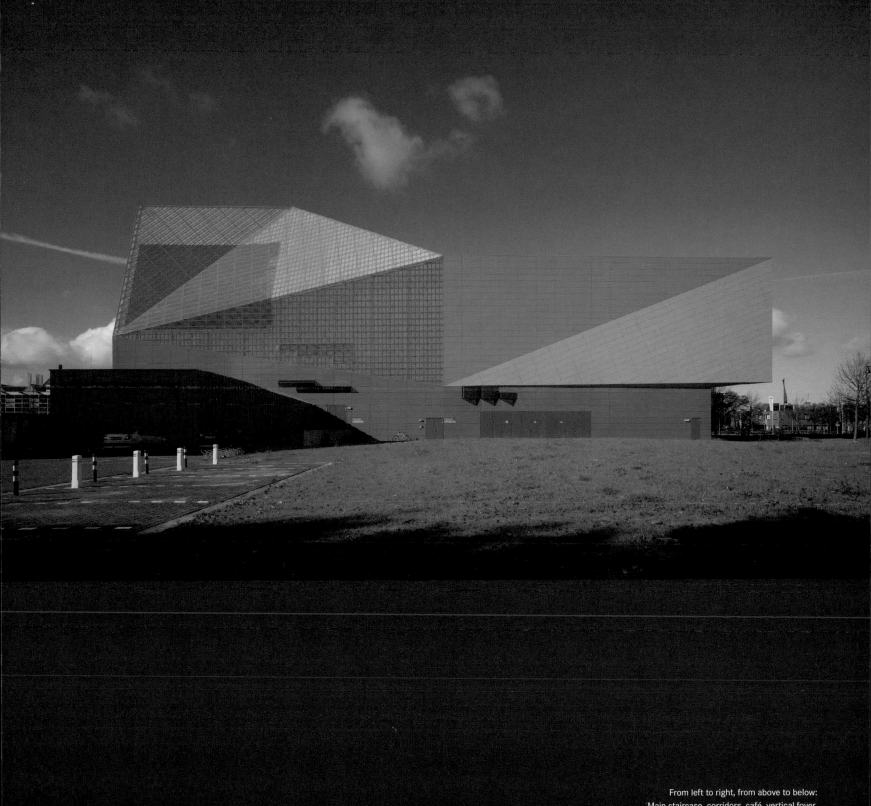

From left to right, from above to below:
Main staircase, corridors, café, vertical foyer.
Right: Façade.

THEATER SNEEK,

SNEEK, THE NETHERLANDS

ALBERTS & VAN HUUT

www.albertsenvanhuut.nl

Type: Theater, opera, ballet, **Setting:** Inner city, **Client:** Municipality Sneek, **Completion:** 2011, **Number of auditoria:** 2, **Number of seats:** 1,000, **Sketches:** Courtesy of Alberts en van Huut, Amsterdam.

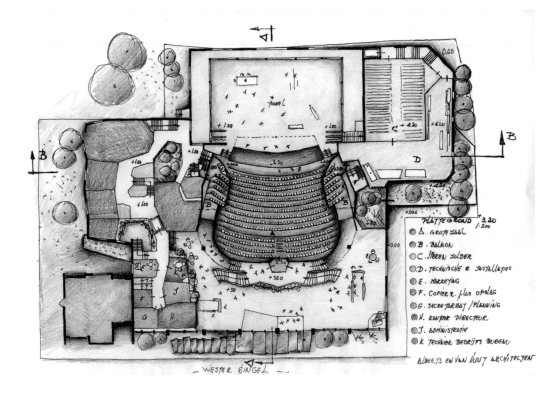

Left: East side. | Right: Second floor plan.

The new 'green' theater in Sneek will be situated in the historic city center. The project consists of a renovation and an extension, adding a total of 600 seats. Adjacent to the foyer, a roof garden offers visitors a place for a break in the open. The theater features perfect acoustics, created by the hall's egg shape, and boasts good sightlines, which together ensure an optimal experience for the viewer. Various patios let daylight into the interior. A number of sustainable technologies, including natural light in the hall and on the stage floor for daytime maintenance, geothermal heat storage, maximization of natural ventilation and ecological materials, such as bamboo composite, were implemented in the structure.

DOORSNEDE: A-A   1:2??

From left to right, from above to below:
The new 'green' theater, roof garden,
panorama of the east side.
Right: Panorama by night.

MUSIC PALACE,
UTRECHT, THE NETHERLANDS

ARCHITECTUURSTUDIO HH

www.ahh.nl

Type: Theater, philharmony, concert halls, **Setting:** Inner city, **Planning partners:** Jo Coenen & Co Archi-
tecten, Architectuurcentrale Thijs Asselbergs, NL Architects, **Original building:** Herman Hertzberger, 1978,
Client: Municipality of Utrecht, **Completion:** 2013, **Number of auditoria:** 5, **Number of seats:** 5,100,
Renderings: UBIKmh and Architectuurstudio HH, Amsterdam.

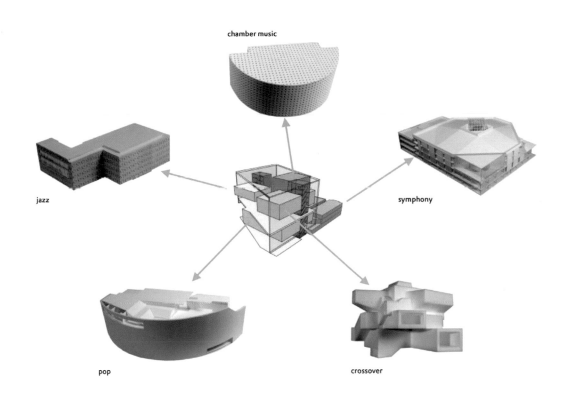

chamber music

jazz

symphony

pop

crossover

Left: South-west side of Music Palace with entrance and grand café. | Right: Main concept.

The Music Palace project is a collaborative venture
of Muziekcentrum Vredenburg, Tivoli and Stichting
Jazz en Geïmproviseerde Muziek. After their joining to
form one company, the diversity of styles will remain.
The design concept's starting point is the bringing
together of five different concert halls under one roof,
whereby each hall, or 'biotope', has its own character.

Hertzberger's existing main auditorium is dedicated to
the symphony biotope; the four new halls will be positioned above or next to the symphony hall, making
their variegated appearance obvious on the exterior
as well as the interior. The pop stage will be designed
by Jo Coenen, the jazz stage by Thijs Asselbergs, and
the cross-over stage, by NL Architects.

From left to right, from above to below:
Entrance, foyer music square,
chamber music hall.
Right: North-west side.

CARTAXO CULTURAL CENTER,
CARTAXO, PORTUGAL

CVDB ARQUITECTOS

www.cvdbarquitectos.com

Type: Theater, opera, ballet, concert hall, **Setting:** Inner city, **Client:** Cartaxo Municipality, **Completion:** 2005, **Number of auditoria:** 2, **Number of seats:** 420, **Additional functions:** Cinema, café, exhibition spaces, workshops, **Photos:** FG + SG – fotografia de arquitectura, Lisbon.

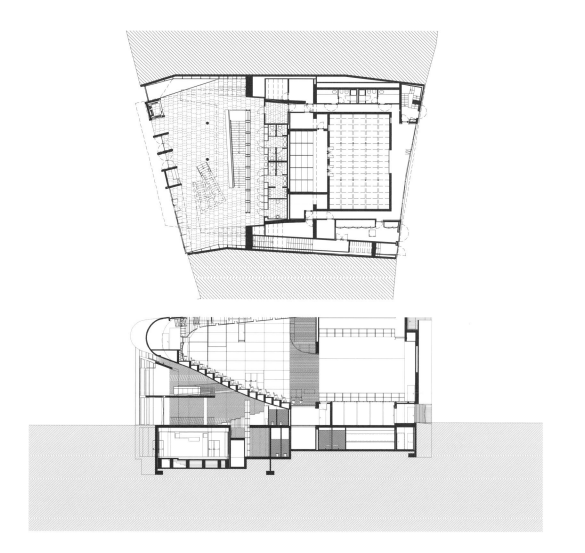

Left: Main façade. | Right: Ground floor plan and section.

The center stands out due to the bold exposed concrete cantilever which projects itself like a belly of a whale onto the street and foyer, sheltering the main auditorium. Sited between two gables, the center introduces an iconographic and public character into the city main square. Transparency and permeability enable a visual and spatial flow and a porous relationship with the square. The foyer is constructed in exposed concrete, natural slate and pine timber studs, emphasizing the natural character of these materials. Strong, bright colors are used in backstage areas to reveal their lively character to the street. In the two halls, light is treated as matter sculptured out of the walls and ceilings surfaces.

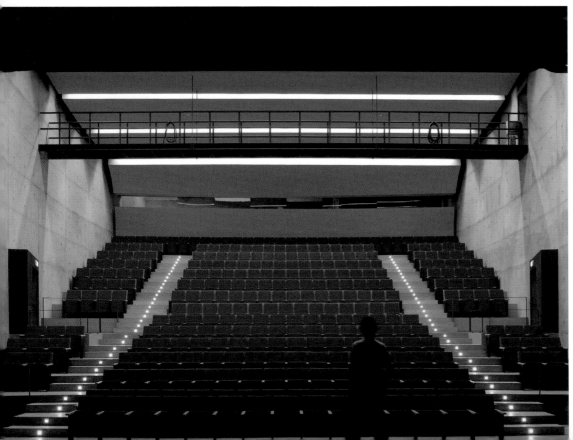

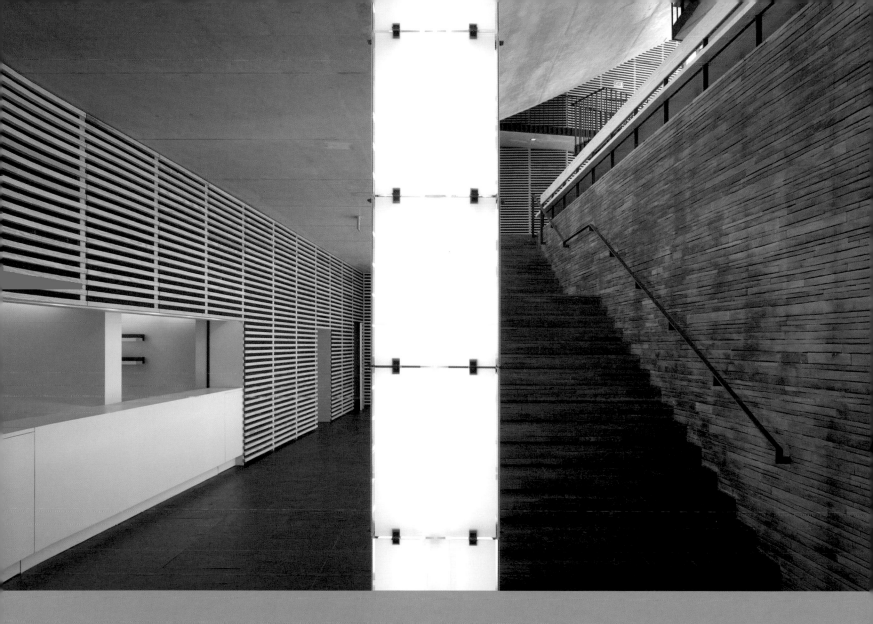

From left to right, from above to below:
View towards the exterior from
the foyer, foyer, auditorium, cinema hall.
Right: Foyer.

MUNICIPAL THEATER,
GUARDA, PORTUGAL

CARLOS VELOSO

www.ava-architects.com

Type: Theater, **Setting:** Urban, **Client:** Guarda municipality, **Completion:** 2005, **Number of auditoria:** 2, **Number of seats:** 787, **Additional functions:** Cinema, living, exhibition, **Photos:** FG+SG Fotografia de arquitetura.

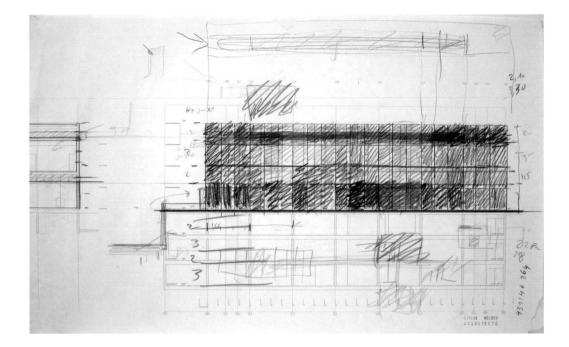

Left: Exterior from north-east. | Right: Façade study.

The building is located in the south of the historic center of Guarda, a town in northern Portugal known for its granite. The theater consists of two volumes of different geometry placed at different levels, which enables staging of outdoor performances. The entrance to each building is defined by changes in soil surface. Ramps isolated from the granite walls, which descend from the street, clearly differentiate the public space and its surroundings and create a unique landscape. The façade openings act as "scene mouths", where the public takes on the role of the scenic action. Spatial organization searches for different viewpoints from the inside to the outside and vise versa.

From left to right, from above to below:
Entrance, stairs, view of the two buildings.
Right: Auditorium.

AUDITORIUM AND CONFERENCE CENTER,
MÉRIDA, SPAIN

NIETO SOBEJANO ARQUITECTOS

www.nietosobejano.com

Type: Theater, opera, ballet, **Setting:** Urban, **Sculptor:** Esther Pizarro, **Client:** Government of Extremadura, **Completion:** 2004, **Number of auditoria:** 2, **Number of seats:** 1,300, **Additional functions:** Exhibition center, **Photos:** © Roland Halbe / artur.

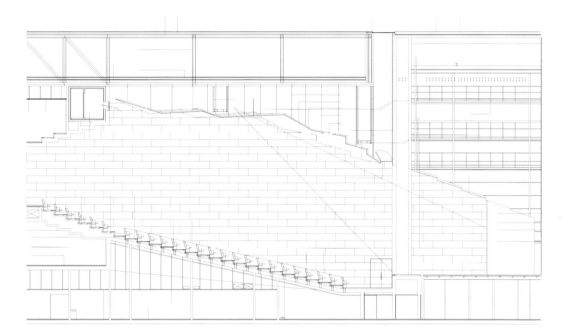

Left: Façade. | Right: Section.

The new center resolves a complex brief, dictating music, theater and opera uses of the auditorium as well as an exhibition pavilion. Additionally, it is also a part of the Guadiana River bank environment with the power and expressiveness required by its public and institutional nature. From the outside, the compact, timeless building is characterized by the continuity of stone-like material, contemporary in its construction technique while at the same time reminiscent of the old Roman walls in Mérida. The main hall has a rectangular plan with an acoustic ceiling of zinc-clad wooden panels, installed independently of the roof structure with a geometry that produces optimal sound conditions.

From left to right, from above to below:
Atrium, exterior by night, perspective view.
Right: Auditorium.

BALUARTE – CONGRESS CENTER AND AUDITORIUM OF NAVARRA,
PAMPLONA, SPAIN

FRANCISCO MANGADO

www.fmangado.com

Type: Theater, opera, ballet, **Setting:** Urban, **Client:** Provincial Government of Navarra, **Completion:** 2003, **Number of auditoria:** 2, **Number of seats:** 1,744, **Photos:** José Manuel Cutillas (224, 226 a. l., 226 b., 227), © Roland Halbe / artur (226 a. r.).

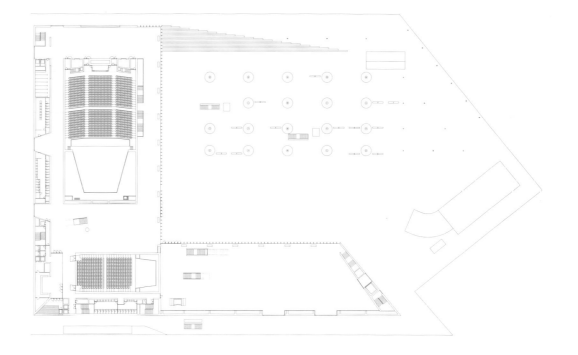

Left: Baluarte on the old fortress. | Right: Ground floor plan.

This project centers around the basic idea of giving up an autonomous architectural scheme in favor of a complex with a clear urban calling. With this in mind, the prisms lock together in an "L" shape, embracing a large square which opens onto the perimeter streets, at the same time establishing a dialog with the former fortress. The two auditoria are autonomous prisms, the larger in one of the shape's arms, the smaller tucked into the angle. The main access and foyer are located between them in a large space which spans the full height of the building, featuring central skylights that illuminate the full depth of the space. Natural tones dominate the interior (light-toned beechwood) and exterior (dark Ipe wood, gray granite, black quartzite).

From left to right, from above to below:
Conference hall, main auditorium, exterior.
Right: Façade.

TENERIFE OPERA HOUSE,
SANTA CRUZ DE TENERIFE, SPAIN

www.calatrava.com

Type: Opera, **Setting:** urban, **Client:** Tenerife Town Council, **Completion:** 2003, **Number of auditoria:** 2, **Number of seats:** Concert hall: 1,660, hall for chamber music: 428, **Additional functions:** Conference center and exhibition hall, **Photos:** Alan Karchmer.

Left: Exterior view. | Right: Sketch.

The most expressive element of the landmark is a free-standing concrete structure known as the Wing. It rises from a 60 meter wide base, sweeps upward in a curve to a height of 60 meters and points toward the Auditorium's new public plaza and the ocean beyond. It rests at three points upon the cone-shaped main body of the Auditorium, which is formed by a double layer of concrete casings. The two outer casings enclose a perimeter hall, while the inner casings enclose the main concert hall, equipped for opera and stage productions. Framing lateral arches made of cylindrical sheets of concrete transmit the loads from the concrete casings to the foundation.

From left to right, from above to below:
Roof, façade detail, foyer, concert hall.
Right: Chamber music hall.

TENERIFE SCHOOL OF DRAMATIC ARTS,
SANTA CRUZ DE TENERIFE, SPAIN

www.gpyarquitectos.com

Type: Theater, **Setting:** Urban, **Client:** Canary Islands Government, Tenerife Island Government, **Completion:** 2003, **Number of auditoria:** variable, **Number of seats:** 300, **Additional functions:** Theater-, film- and dance-workshops, **Photos:** Teresa Arozena, gpy arquitectos (232, 234 a. l.), Efraín Pintos, gpy arquitectos (234 a. r., 234 b. r.), Manuel Medina (234 b. l.), Miguel de Guzmán / www.imagensubliminal.com (235).

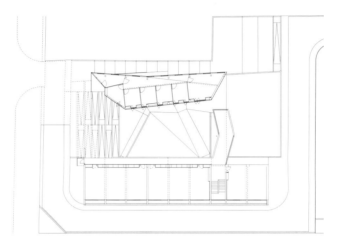

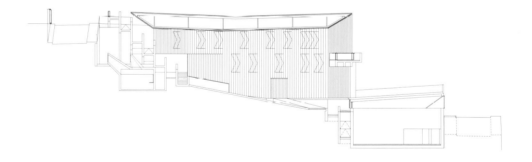

Left: Patio with open-air auditorium. | Right: Floor plan second level and section patio.

This center for the dramatic arts presents itself to the city as a platform, with the city and the landscape acting as a backdrop. The interior roofed patio generated by a three-dimensional folding of the wooden surface of the roof, is conceived as a scenic box that opens up towards the city and affirms itself as the building's spatial reference point, a place for relationships and interchange, where the action, as it unfolds, defines the space of representation. Defined as an inclined surface, the patio functions at the same time as an open-air auditorium and as the backbone for the pedestrian routes throughout the building. These communication routes consist of a system of ramps that connect the building's scenic spaces via an oblique zigzag geometry.

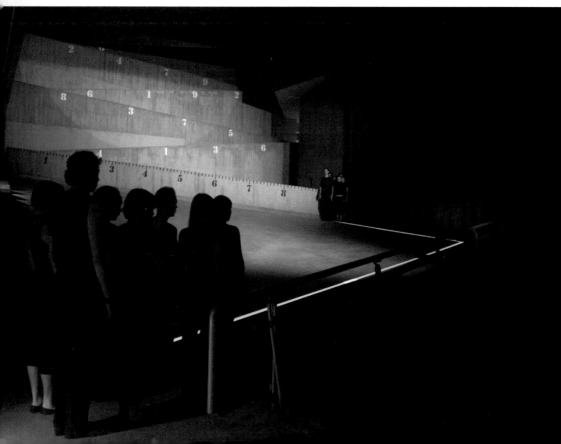

From left to right, from above to below:
Patio, main terrace and open-air stage,
performance, rehearsal room
and flexible performance space.
Right: Interior view.

VALENCIA OPERA HOUSE (PALAU DE LES ARTS),
VALENCIA, SPAIN

www.calatrava.com

Type: Opera, **Setting:** Urban, **Client:** Generalitat Valenciana and City of Arts and Science, S.A., **Completion:** 2006, **Number of auditoria:** 4, **Number of seats:** 4,006, **Photos:** Barbara Burg + Oliver Schuh / Palladium Photodesign (236, 238), Alan Karchmer (239).

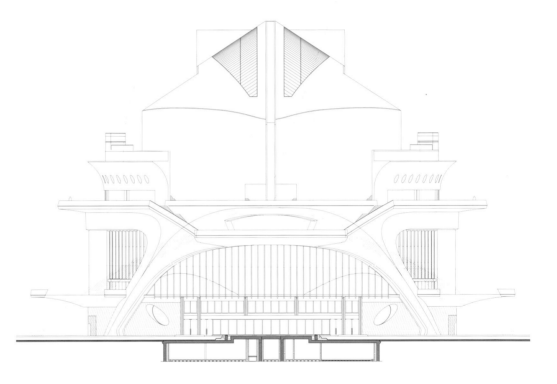

Left: Exterior view. | Right: Section.

Serving all kinds of performing arts, the venue is the final element in the City of Arts and Sciences complex, designed by Calatrava on an 86-acre site along the dry bed of a river. In recognition of the importance of the Opera House, the building has the iconographic character of a monumental sculpture. A series of apparently random volumes are united by being enclosed within two symmetrical cut-away concrete shells, crowned by a sweeping steel sheath. The shell surrounding the building allows peripheral exterior circulation to reach the different auditoriums, garden terraces, cafeterias and the restaurant. Linked by promenade balconies, stairs and exterior elevators, they all offer beautiful views of the city and the gardens.

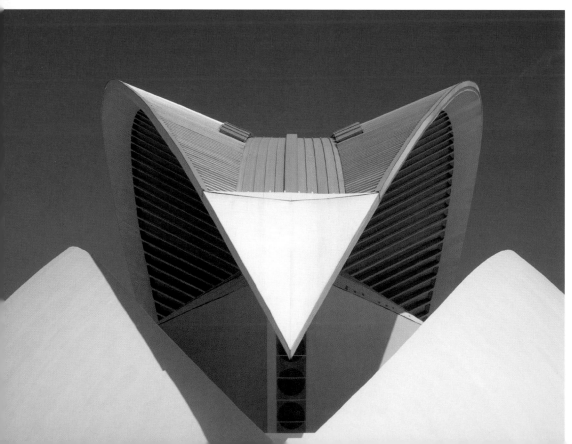

From left to right, from above to below:
Detail façade, promenade decks, detail roof, balconies.
Right: Auditorium.

239

MONDIAL CULTURAL MUSIC THEATRE,
YVERDON-LES-BAINS, SWITZERLAND

HOLZER KOBLER ARCHITEKTUREN /
TRISTAN KOBLER AND
BARBARA HOLZER

www.holzerkobler.ch

Type: Theater music club, **Setting:** Suburban park, **Planning partners:** Hans-Rudolf Rast (Expo.02), **Interior design:** SLS-Illusion + Construction, Schwerzenbach, **Client:** Expo.02, **Completion:** 2002, **Number of auditoria:** 1, **Number of seats:** 400, **Additional functions:** Bar, restaurant, VIP-Lounge, **Photos:** Courtesy of Holzer Kobler Architekturen, Zurich.

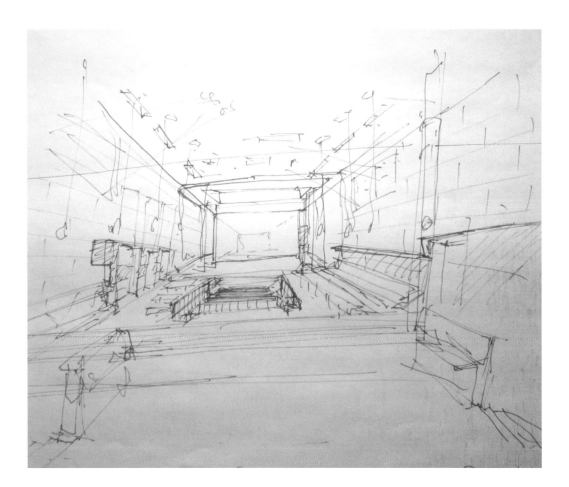

Left: North façade. | Right: Sketch.

Mondial, the Expo.02 world music and theater club, is located on the Arteplage Yverdon-les-Bains. The name is programmatic. The Mondial welcomes guests from around the world to the Swiss national exhibition according to the "I and the universe" Arteplage motto. The building creates an atomspheric envelope for the living, colorful interior, which gives an impression of having always been there. Fascinating found objects from each guest country are exhibited at the entrance. The interior of the Mondial offers many different options for performances with its seperate levels (stage, bar and restaurant) and flexible furniture, nicely accompanied by its offering of world music and eclectic foods.

From left to right, from above to below:
View to stage, exterior by night, stage, entrance area.
Right: North façade.

WEI-WU-YING CENTER
FOR THE PERFORMING ARTS,
KAOHSIUNG, TAIWAN

MECANOO ARCHITECTEN

www.mecanoo.nl

Type: Concert hall, recital, **Setting:** Urban, **Client:** Council for Cultural Affairs, Taiwan, **Completion:** 2013, **Number of auditoria:** 4, **Number of seats:** 5,900, **Additional functions:** Outdoor seating/theater, rehearsal spaces, dance and orchestra, parking, restaurant, offices, library, **Renderings:** Mecanoo architecten.

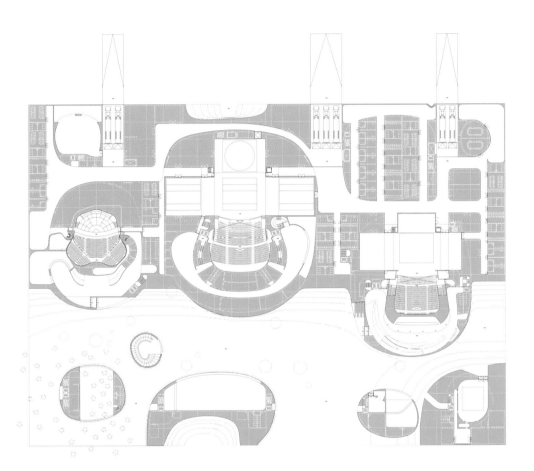

Left: Exterior. | Right: Ground floor plan.

The complex features a concert hall, an opera house, a theater, a recital hall and an open air theater. Hosting 5,900 seats and the most technologically advanced theater facilities, the National Performing Arts Center will become the new icon of the city of Kaohsiung. The center is part of the Wei-Wu-Ying Metropolitan Park, featuring centuries-old banyan trees on location which provided inspiration for the building complex. With the help of openings in the roof, multiple passageways and open spaces, an almost porous building has been created, where the interior and exterior blur together. The roof creates natural and efficient building cooling in the subtropical climate, additionally serving as an informal public space.

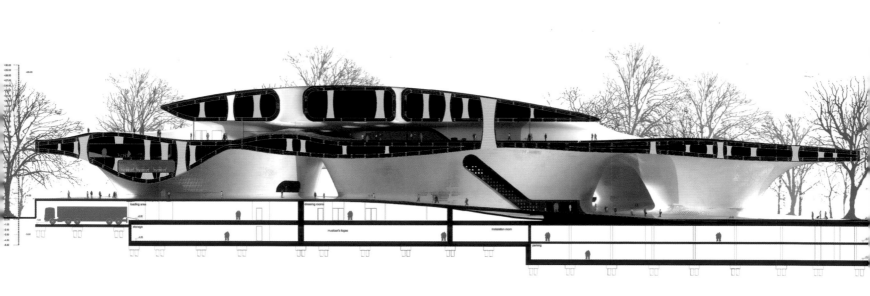

From left to right, from above to below:
Section, concert hall, foyer playhouse.
Right: Banyan Plaza.

TAIPEI PERFORMING ARTS CENTER,
TAIPEI, TAIWAN

OFFICE FOR METROPOLITAN ARCHITECTURE (OMA)

www.OMA.nl

Type: Theater, **Setting:** Urban, **Stage design:** Ducks Sceno, **Client:** Department of Cultural Affairs, Taipei City Government, **Completion:** 2014, **Number of auditoria:** 3, **Number of seats:** 3,100, **Renderings and photos:** OMA (248, 250 a. r., 250 b., 251), OMA / Frans Parthesius (250 a. l.).

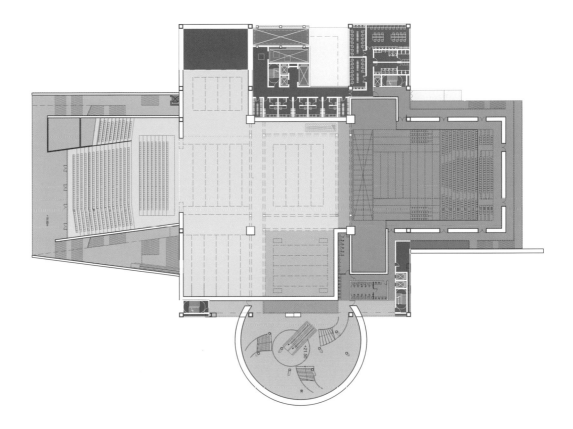

Left: Interior. | Right: Floor plan.

The center includes a 1,500-seat theater and two 800-seat theaters which plug into a central corrugated glass-clad cube sheltering stage accommodations for all three theaters. Each auditorium may be used independently or in combination, which opens new, experimental theatrical possibilities. A public trajectory inside the cube partially exposes backstage areas, which usually remain hidden in typical theaters. The cube is placed on a plinth, preserving the local food market which has existed in the area for years. The Taipei city council expects the center to facilitate the development of local performing groups and add to Taipei's image as an international cultural hub.

CURVE,
LEICESTER, UNITED KINGDOM

www.rvapc.com

Type: Theater, **Setting:** Inner city, **Client:** Leicester Theatre Trust and Leicester City Council, **Completion:** 2008, **Number of auditoria:** 2, **Number of seats:** 1,100, **Photos:** Peter Cook (252, 254 b., 255), Will Pryce (254 a. l., 254 a. r.).

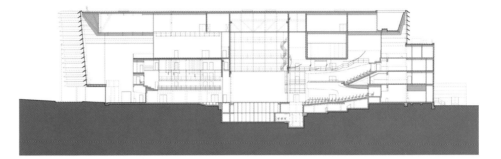

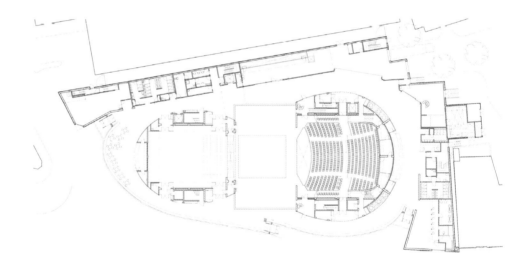

Left: Façade. | Right: Section and ground floor plan.

'Curve' is an innovative, democratic building which respects Leicester's history, while helping to redefine its future. The cutting-edge design turns the typical theater configuration 'inside out' by exposing all components of the theater to the public and integrating all aspects of performance into the life of the city. For the very first time, audiences and passers-by will be engaged in the actual process of theater-making, behind the scenes. Conceived as islands within a public foyer, a central stage sits at street level between two colored volumes, and a system of metal shutters enables the creative team to place the audience in a variety of configurations, creating possibilities for either conventional or technically more ambitious theater production and design.

From left to right, from above to below:
Façade, interior theater, interior shot.
Right: Interior.

ROYAL SHAKESPEARE THEATRE,
STRATFORD-UPON-AVON, UNITED KINGDOM

BENNETTS ASSOCIATES ARCHITECTS

www.bennettsassociates.com

Type: Theater, **Setting:** Rural, **Landscape architect:** Nicholas Pearson Associates, **Interior design:** Charcoalblue (theater consultant), **Client:** Royal Shakespeare Company, **Original building:** 1879–1932, **Completion:** 2010, **Number of auditoria:** 2, **Number of seats:** Royal Shakespeare Theater: 1,040, Swan Theater: 450, **Additional functions:** Café, bars, restaurant, tower with viewing gallery, muti-purpose workshop/admin space, **Renderings:** RSC/Cityscape (256, 258 a. l., 258 a. r., 258 b. l.), RSC/Hayes Davidson (258 b. r., 259).

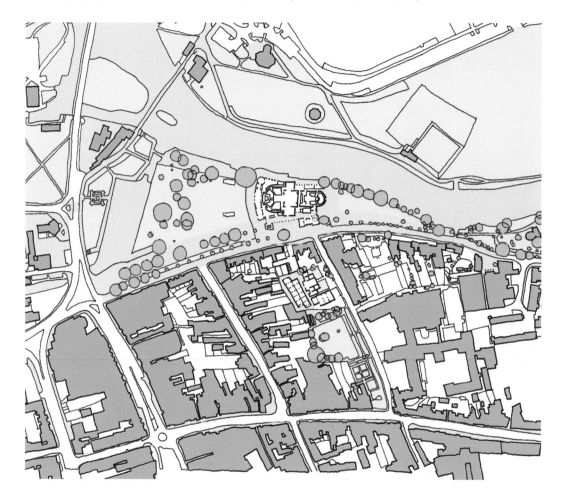

Left: A reworking of the building beside the River Avon. | Right: Site plan

Central to the project is a thrust-format, galleried performance space for just over 1,000 seats to replace the present fan-shaped auditorium, which has suffered from acoustic and sightline difficulties since its construction in the early 1930s. A new multi-level foyer envelopes the new auditorium, releasing the retained art-deco rooms facing the Bancroft Gardens for additional café space and interval bars. A new panoramic restaurant on the third floor replaces a later addition to the original building, revealing the full extent of the original river façade. Facing the city, a glazed colonnade connects the two theaters. Together with the existing picture gallery, the tower and the colonnade define a new public square that acts as a gathering point and an outdoor performance venue.

From left to right, from above to below:
Building beside the River Avon, façade, view from Bancroft
Gardens, cutaway axonometr ic showing refurbishment.
Right: Sectional perspective through new seating and stage.

THE ARBOUR – YORKSHIRE FORWARD
RENAISSANCE PAVILION,
VARIOUS SITES, YORKSHIRE, UNITED KINGDOM

LOCK RENNIE LLP

www.lockrennie.com

Type: Concert hall, **Setting:** Various sites, **Client:** Yorkshire Forward, **Completion:** 2010, **Number of auditoria:** 1, **Number of seats:** 200, **Additional functions:** Café, lectures, workshops, meals, debates, exhibitions and film screenings, **Renderings:** Lock Rennie LLP.

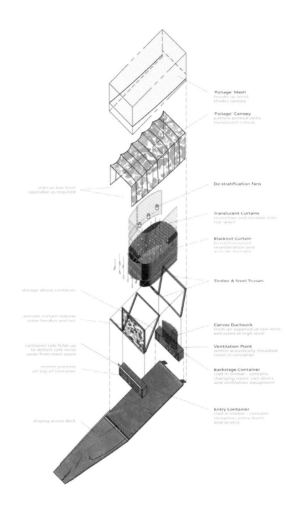

Left: Architects' impression of a show in the Arbour. | Right: Components of the Arbour.

The Arbour is a demountable pavilion for an audience of 200. It accommodates events like concerts, lectures, exhibitions and film screenings throughout the Yorkshire region and the United Kingdom. It is conceived as a modern arbor, a manmade clearing within trees which brings the landscape into the city, and inserts shelter into its chosen landscape. The Arbour is accessed from a sloping external deck which can be positioned to relate to the local context: a long linear form responding to the landscape or an 'L' shape. Lightweight translucent PVC fabrics were used to act as structural elements. Two fabric layers create a light and floating rectilinear external form, which contrasts with the baroque-like interior.

From left to right, from above to below:
Model showing public entry deck, entrance and café,
interior, architects' impression of
the Arbour in Leeds' Millenium Square.
Right: Architects' impression
of the pavilion on Scarborough beach.

RICHARD B. FISHER CENTER FOR THE PERFORMING ARTS AT BARD COLLEGE,

ANNANDALE-ON-HUDSON, NY, USA

GEHRY PARTNERS, LLP

www.foga.com

Type: Theater, opera, ballet, concert, **Setting:** Rural, **Design acoustics:** Yasuhisa Toyota, **Client:** Bard College, **Completion:** 2003, **Number of auditoria:** 2, **Number of seats:** All: 1,100, main auditorium: 900, **Additional functions:** Dance studios, **Photos:** © Roland Halbe / artur.

Left: Main auditorium Sosnoff Theater. | Right: Sketch.

The unusual form of the outer building results from the inner sequence of the two performance spaces, stage tower and the remaining structural elements, swept over by a brushed stainless steel plate. Draped like a cloth, the plate reflects the surroundings from varying angles. The Sosnoff Theater designed by Gehry together with the acoustic designer Yasuhisa Toyota is a first-class concert hall which invites experimental performances with its unusual architectural context. Additional program includes Theater Two with a semi-fly tower and the Felicitas S. Thorne Dance Studio, a laboratory for young dancers and choreographers.

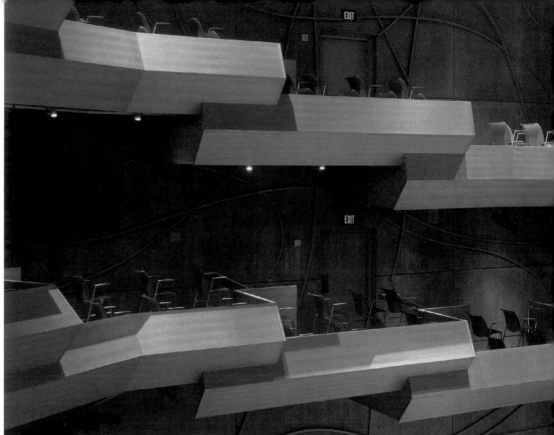

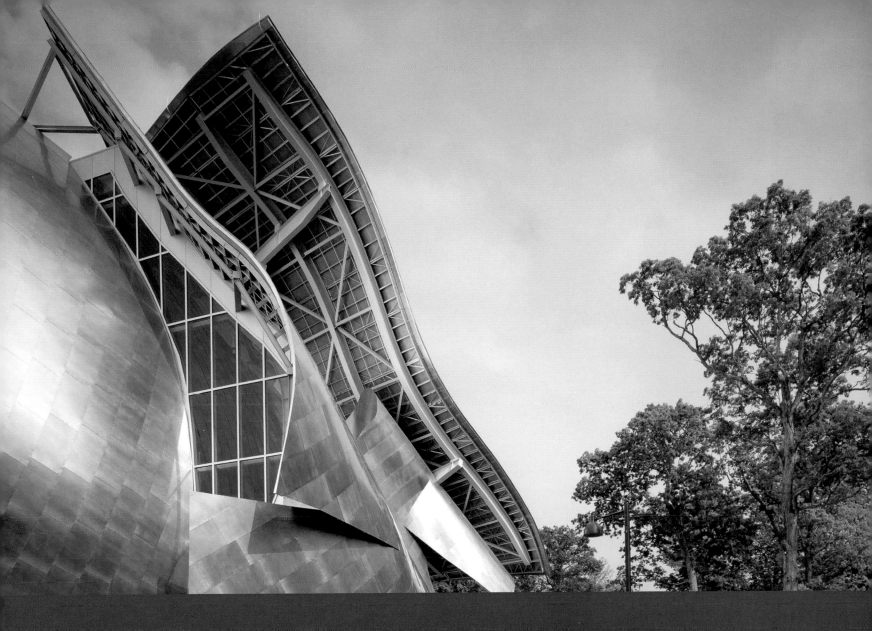

From left to right, from above to below:
Foyer, balconies and acoustic elements
on the wall, exterior from south-east.
Right: Detail north-west façade.

DEE AND CHARLES WYLY THEATER,
DALLAS, TX, USA

OFFICE FOR METROPOLITAN ARCHITECTURE (OMA)

www.OMA.nl

Type: Theater, **Setting:** Inner city, **Client:** Dallas Center for the Performing Arts, **Completion:** 2009, **Number of auditoria:** 1, **Number of seats:** 575, **Additional functions:** Administrative offices, rehearsal spaces, café, gift shop, cocktail bar, **Photos:** Iwan Baan.

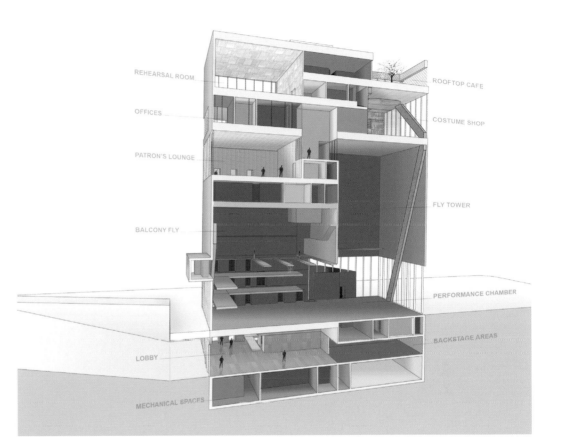

REHEARSAL ROOM

ROOFTOP CAFE

OFFICES

COSTUME SHOP

PATRON'S LOUNGE

FLY TOWER

BALCONY FLY

PERFORMANCE CHAMBER

BACKSTAGE AREAS

LOBBY

MECHANICAL SPACES

Left: Exterior by night. | Right: Program sceme.

The compact, vertical orientation of the 12-story-high Dee and Charles Wyly Theater stacks supporting spaces, such as the foyer, ticket counters and backstage facilities, above and beneath the auditorium, instead of having them wrap around it. This re-imagining of the theater typology exposes the auditorium to the city on all sides. Shakespeare can be performed in a hermetic container, or – by simply opening the blackout blinds along the exterior glass walls – with the city of Dallas as a backdrop. The form also facilitates innovation in the theater's mechanics: the conventional fly tower above the stage has been vertically extended and can pull up both scenery and seating.

From left to right, from above to below:
View from the upper evel outdoor terrace, café, auditorium.
Right: Theater with visible auditorium.

WINSPEAR OPERA HOUSE,
DALLAS, TX, USA

www.fosterandpartners.com

Type: Opera, ballet, musical, **Setting:** Urban, **Planning partners:** Kendall / Heaton, **Client:** Dallas Center for the Performing Arts Foundation, **Completion:** 2009, **Number of auditoria:** 1, **Number of seats:** 2,200, **Additional functions:** Outdoor performance space, **Photos:** Foster + Partners (272, 274 b., 275), Nigel Young / Foster + Partners (274 a. l., 274 a. r).

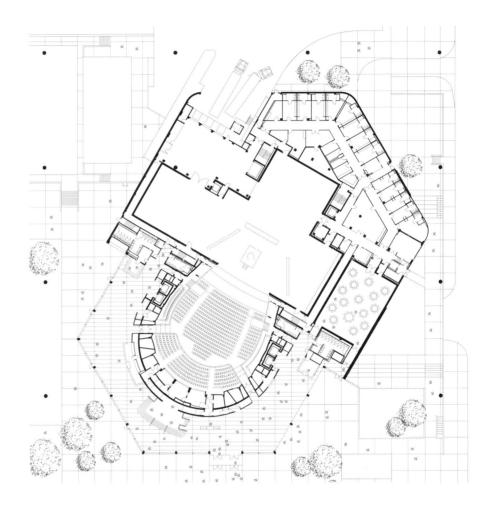

Left: Entrance area. | Right: Floor plan.

This part of the Dallas Center for the Performing Arts will be home to The Dallas Opera, Texas Ballet Theater, touring Broadway productions and numerous other performances. It redefines the essence of an opera house, breaking down barriers to make opera more accessible to a wider audience. A generous solar canopy extends from the building, revealing a fully glazed sixty-foot-high lobby and the rich red glass drum of the 2,200-seat auditorium below. Angled off-grid under the canopy, there are two outdoor performance spaces, a café terrace and the main entrance to the opera house. Vertical sliding glass panels, movable across the full length of the east façade, allow the building with a café and restaurant to be fully opened up.

From left to right, from above to below:
Foyer, entrance, façade.
Right: In the auditorium.

IRVINE VALLEY COLLEGE PERFORMING ARTS CENTER,
IRVINE, CA, USA

ARQUITECTONICA

www.arquitectonica.com

Type: Theater, ballet, **Setting:** Urban, **Client:** Irvine Valley College, **Completion:** 2007, **Number of auditoria:** 3, **Number of seats:** All: 550, main auditorium: 400, **Photos:** Paul Turang, Long Beach.

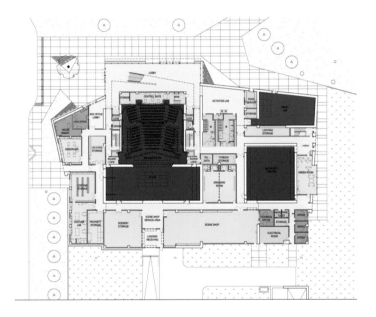

Left: View looking south-east. | Right: First floor plan.

Situated directly on the edge of the campus, this performing arts center was specifically catered to the wishes and needs of students and faculty members. The building includes three departments, one for each of the faculties – drama, dance and music. The main hall with 400 seats and a balcony created around the orchestra was designed for varied use. In addition, the building includes a music hall with 50 seats and a black box experimental theater with 100 seats, which together allow for flexible and innovative productions. The varied façade with an eye-catching structure matches the diversity and vitality of the action taking place inside. The walls of the entrance area feature large glass fronts which let light into the foyer.

From left to right, from above to below:
Lobby, view of reception lobby from north,
main stage, reception lobby interior.
Right: Main stage.

MESA ARTS CENTER,
MESA, AZ, USA

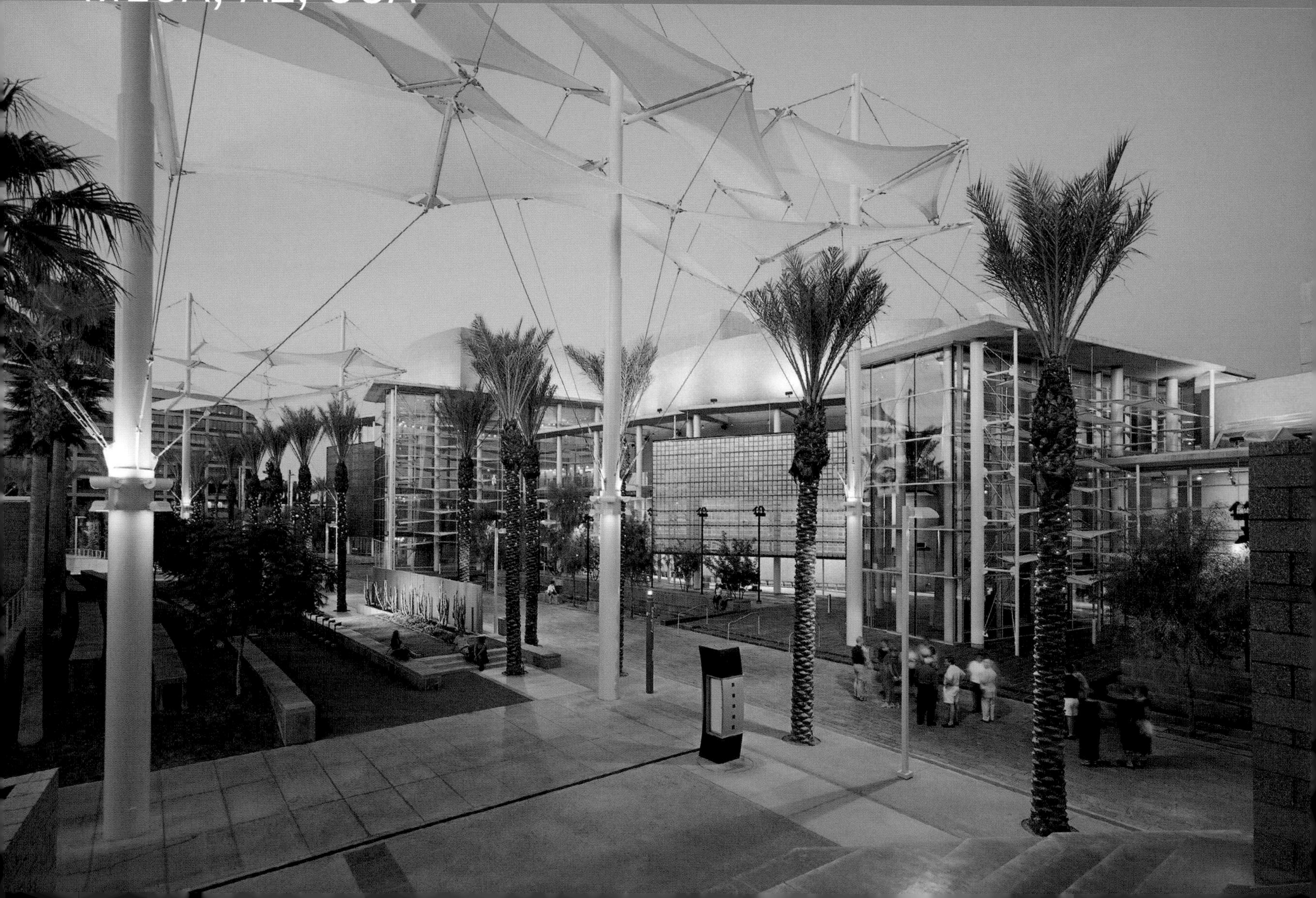

BOORA ARCHITECTS AND
DWL ARCHITECTS + PLANNERS

www.boora.com, www.dwlarchitects.com

Type: Theater, **Setting:** Inner city, **Landscape architect:** Martha Schwarz Partners, **Client:** Mesa Arts Center, **Completion:** 2005, **Number of auditoria:** 4, **Number of seats:** All: 2,438, main auditorium: 1,588, **Additional functions:** Visual art studios, contemporary art gallery, public plaza, **Photos:** Timothy Hursley/ Little Rock.

Left: Public plaza at night with theaters beyond. | Right: First floor plan with site plan.

The Mesa Arts Center with its four theaters, arts education center and contemporary gallery is the most comprehensive arts complex in the region. It offers an expansive performance program of regional companies and touring entertainment, as well as studio arts and exhibitions. Its architecture proposes a dynamic alternative to the predominantly low, sprawling city. Each hall is expressed as an independent volume in the bold colors of the Sonoran Desert landscape. The fly towers are canted in gesture to the mountains surrounding the Phoenix Basin. A public plaza at the heart of the Mesa Arts Center offers a shaded, multi-layered gathering place for citizens and event goers.

From left to right, from above to below:
Ikeda Theater, Piper Repertory Theater, Ikeda Theater.
Right: Water feature in the plaza.

GUTHRIE THEATER,
MINNEAPOLIS, MN, USA

ATELIERS JEAN NOUVEL

www.jeannouvel.com

Type: Theater, **Setting:** Urban, **Client:** The Guthrie Theater, **Completion:** 2006, **Number of auditoria:** 3, **Number of seats:** 2,050, **Photos:** Philippe Ruault (284, 286 a., 286 b. l., 287), © Roland Halbe / artur (286 b. r.)

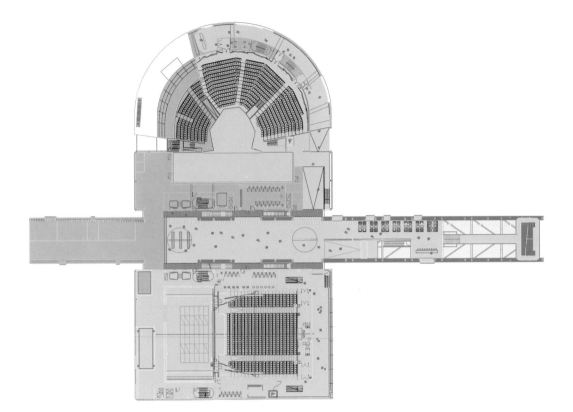

Left: Looking through the window of the museum. | Right: Floor plan fourth floor.

In the early 1960s Tyrone Guthrie created a theater festival dedicated to the classics, seen as an alternative to Broadway. Today, the Guthrie is a focal point in the cultural life of Minneapolis. The new Guthrie Theater stands on the shore of the Mississippi in the historic mill district, surrounded by the mills and silos which had made an impression on Walter Gropius, Le Corbusier and Moisei Ginzburg. The building captures the silhouette without pastiche. Its smooth facing material, clear, stark outlines, and somber hues set it apart. In a register all its own, it blends in while simultaneously contrasting with the surroundings. The orange lobby, a nod to traditional mill signs, stands guard over the landscape.

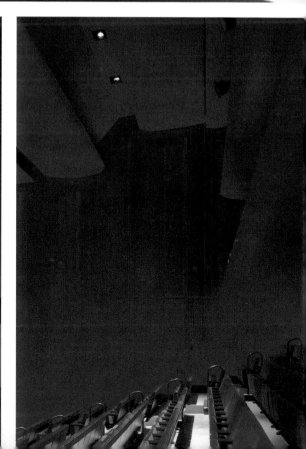

From left to right, from above to below:
Window in the "orange box" on level 9,
window in blue glass at the end of the cantilever bridge, cantilever
bridge, Proscenium Stage.
Right: Theater in the Minneapolis mill district.

THE ELI AND EDYTHE BROAD STAGE,
SANTA MONICA, CA, USA

RENZO ZECCHETTO ARCHITECTS

www.zecchetto.com

Type: Theater, opera, ballet, **Setting:** Urban, **Client:** Santa Monica College, **Completion:** 2005, **Number of auditoria:** 2, **Number of seats:** 498, **Additional functions:** Cinema, lecture hall, **Photos:** Benny Chan, fotoworks, Los Angeles (288, 290/291, 292 a. l., 292 a. r., 293), Robert Berger Photography (292 b. l.), Renzo Zecchetto Architects, Santa Monica (292 b. r.).

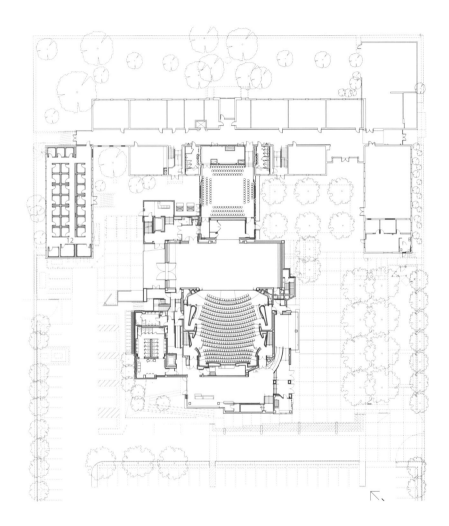

Left: Auditorium. | Right: Site plan.

The Broad Stage is a state-of-the-art, 540-seat theater in Santa Monica which provides an astonishing venue for the performing arts. A large, cantilevered overhang marks the entry plaza which serves as both a gathering space and an outdoor extension to the lobby. On the evening of a performance, the wood-clad shell of the house is illuminated like a softly glowing lantern. The space between the house shell and the glass curtain wall forms a soaring lobby. In the auditorium, acoustic considerations inspired the use of convex plaster wall elements and sculpted mahogany panels, arranged to both distribute the sound to the audience and to form layered pockets for lighting and box seating.

South-west elevation.

From left to right, from above to below:
Lobby, proscenium from main balcony,
view from proscenium boxes,
ticketbooth and entry at night.
Right: Night view.

WESTMINSTER ROSE CENTER,
WESTMINSTER, CA, USA

CO ARCHITECTS

www.coarchitects.com

Type: Theater, **Setting:** Urban, **Client:** City of Westminster, **Completion:** 2006, **Number of auditoria:** 1, **Number of seats:** 420, **Additional functions:** Venue for banquets and ceremonies, space for exhibition and meetings, **Photos:** Benny Chan, Fotoworks Los Angeles.

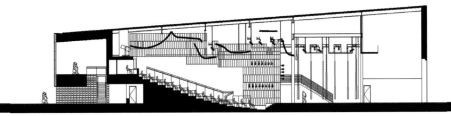

Section Through Theater

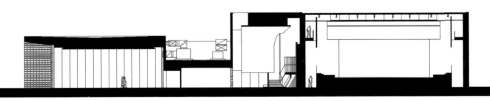

Section

Left: Theater echelons. | Right: Sections.

CO Architects used innovative glazing on the façade to establish the Rose Center's presence. Two main glass volumes balance adjacent masonry-clad volumes and transform them into a dramatic, glowing entry beacon. Three types of glass – clear, fritted and patterned – create a variety of transparencies and textures while defining the volumes that house the entry and the theater. The façade's scrim-like effect communicates the building's function as a theater and performing arts center. An elegant 600-foot-long plaza progresses toward the main foyer, a soaring, triangular volume inserted between the theater and the banquet facility. The space's simplicity makes it easily adaptable for a variety functions, including use as an art gallery.

From left to right, from above to below:
Concrete masonry and glass continuing into the interior, glass
façade illuminated at night, elemental colors continuing into the
theater, irregularly patterned glass resemble bamboo plants.
Right: Elevation from Freedom Park.

MARK TAPER FORUM,
LOS ANGELES, CA, USA

RIOS CLEMENTI HALE STUDIOS

www.rchstudios.com

Type: Theater, **Setting:** Urban, **Planning partners:** Harley Ellis Deveraux, **Original building:** Welton Becket, 1967, **Client:** The Music Center of Los Angeles County, **Completion:** 2008, **Number of auditoria:** 1, **Number of seats:** 739, **Additional functions:** Lobby, lounge, greenroom, **Photos:** Tom Bonner.

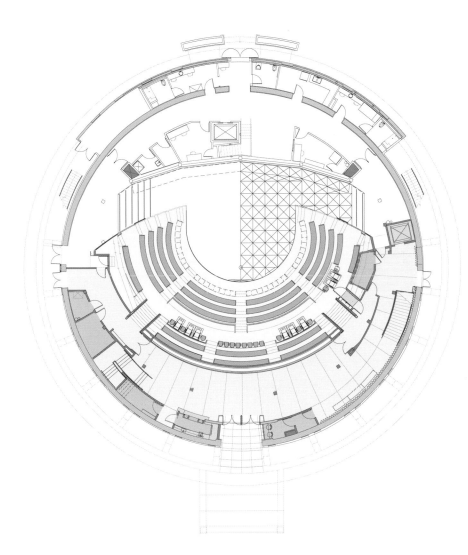

Left: Façade. | Right: Plaza level floor plan.

The Mark Taper Forum was subject to an interior renovation with a complete refurbishment reaching from the lobby to the seating. In addition to receiving a modern design update, it was also provided with elements to improve audience comfort. New, larger restrooms and a comfortable lounge area, accessible by both elevator and stairs, were added. The backstage area with dressing rooms, wardrobes and other spaces was extended in order to ameliorate the working conditions for performers and staff. The curved mosaic wall in the lobby is now showcased by lighting effects. The key elements of the exterior architecture, however, were kept in order to maintain the building's character.

Brindell and Milton Gottlieb - Act

From left to right, from above to below:
Stairways, mosaic wall,
exterior from east, lounge.
Right: Auditorium.

INDEX.